1—

A Few Stout Individuals

JOHN GUARE

A Few Stout Individuals

A play in two acts

Grove Press
New York

Published simultaneously in Canada
Printed in the United States of America

FIRST EDITION

Library of Congress Cataloging-in-Publication Data

Guare, John.
    A few stout individuals / by John Guare.
       p. cm.
    ISBN 0-8021-4002-5
     1. Grant, Ulysses S. (Ulysses Simpson), 1822–1885—Drama. 2. Throat—Cancer—
Patients—Drama. 3. Autobiography—Authorship—Drama. 4. New York (N.Y.)—
Drama. 5. Generals—Drama. I. Title.
PS3557.U2F49 2003
812'.54—dc21   2002041675

Grove Press
841 Broadway
New York, NY 10003

03 04 05 06 07   10 9 8 7 6 5 4 3 2 1

for Karel Reisz

(1926–2002)

and life at Chalcot Gardens

PREFACE

A few years ago, someone asked me if I had read Ulysses S. Grant's *Personal Memoirs*. I said, "Of course not." This person, whom I did not know, said, "And you call yourself an educated person?" I huffed away. The horrible things you have to put up with at cocktail parties. But it stung me.

I'm not totally ignorant. I had once peeked into the *Memoirs* a few years earlier while doing research for a series of plays called *Lydie Breeze* that I was writing about the Civil War and its aftermath. The first play in the series, called *Women and Water,* opened at the battle of Cold Harbor, one of the most bloodthirsty, blood-curdling battles in that war and one that haunted its survivors for the rest of their lives. Grant had been in charge. Grant became the symbol of drunken corruption and waste, the very nemesis of, the personification of evil for my characters who had suffered under him. In my glance into the *Memoirs,* I saw that Grant had written about the disgrace of Cold Harbor. "I have always regretted that the last assault at Cold Harbor was ever made. At Cold Harbor no advantage whatever was gained to compensate for the heavy loss we sustained." That's all he said. Back then I didn't need to know any more about the man. My characters needed to hate him. I followed their lead . . .

But that stranger must have stung me more deeply than I thought, for, a while later, I was in my home away from home, New York City's indispensible Strand Bookstore, when I came upon a beat-up copy of Grant's *Personal Memoirs*. I bought it. I read it. I had a very unsettling experience reading this remarkable document. I felt I was hearing—how to put it?—the twentieth century beating its fists against the nineteenth-century typeface of his book, as if the print itself were a prison cage with these prescient fists beating against it, saying, Hear me. That's a pretty

vii

florid reaction, you might say. But the book bowled me over. What got me was not a nineteenth-century voice, but that you could hear Gertrude Stein in its locutions. You could hear Hemingway in its simplicity and directness. I finished the book with a profound respect for Grant, so much so that I had to know how this supposedly drunken general, this corrupt president, wrote such a masterpiece—for a masterpiece it is.

The story told in this play is the story I found. I couldn't believe the cast of characters that produced this work—including Samuel Clemens as publisher—or the circumstances under which the book was written. In 1885 Grant and his wife were living at 3 East Sixty-sixth Street, right off Fifth Avenue in New York City. Here was a once great man, disgraced by an Enron-size scandal not of his own making, which rendered him penniless and ruined, as well, a lot of New Yorkers who'd invested their money in Grant's investment bank on the strength of his involvement in it. Grant's shame and ruin were enormous. Clemens came to the rescue. He would publish the memoirs along with *Huckleberry Finn* and make a fortune for everyone involved. Grant, who had resisted ever writing about the war, was forced to write these memoirs to earn money for his destitute family. He was battling throat cancer, leg injuries, dental butchery, and was kept heavily drugged against the pain. I imagined Clemens returning from a long reading tour across America to find an author who couldn't remember, a man who had lost his memory forced to remember. It seemed Grant's nightmare experience of producing his memoirs became a compressed metaphor for the very act of writing. How much of the making of any play or book or painting or piece of music is the scary result of chance, luck, persistence, health, timing, inspiration—grace. This story reminded me how fragile the act of creation is and the perilousness of memory. In this age of confession and big-buck memoirs, Grant was the first and still is the king in terms of sales and numbers of copies printed. This story haunted me. Grant's nobility of spirit surprised me and pleased me. I couldn't believe that no one had written this story yet.

But how do you tell such a story, whose main character is semiconscious and in agonizing pain? I put the play on the back burner. But I was now hooked on Grant. I found a remarkable two-volume work published in 1879 called *Around the World with General Grant,* by John Russell Young. Toward the end of his travels after he left the presidency in 1870, Grant arrived in Japan and met the young emperor, Meiji, who revered him. He gave Grant a hero's welcome and even had a Noh play written and performed in his honor at a legendary banquet. Grant enjoyed the play so much that it sparked a revival of interest in the dying art of the Noh in Japan that has continued to this day. Grant shone in Japan. This could possibly have been the happiest Grant and his wife ever were. The period of the memoir writing was the lowest. How to put these times together? I had the style of the play.

Usually I don't work off research. The richness of the period of 1885 was so compelling, and yet the details were drowning me. Adelina Patti was appearing in New York at that time. How to use that? I would sit at my desk trying to find my way into the play. I owed James Houghton and the Signature Theater a play, commissioned for spring 2002. I hoped this would be it. James Houghton said that he didn't need to see the play yet, but he did need to announce it, and he had to have a title and synopsis, some tag for the ads. Title. Title. Okay. Emerson said, "What is history but the biography of a few stout individuals?" That was my title. A synopsis for an ad? I gave him the following: "A great man is dying penniless, his son having squandered his fortune. A publisher offers the great man a fortune to write his memoirs. How will the family keep him alive to finish them? How will the great man get to his memory?" No mention of U. S. Grant or Clemens. Donald Moffat, an actor I admire tremendously, called me the day after the ad was printed in the *Times.* "I'd love to play that man," he said. "All right," I said. "As soon as I finish it, I'll send it to you." But I couldn't find a way into the play. I had a title. I had a lead. I had a production announcement. I had no play. I had lots of material but no magnet underneath to hold it together.

And then September 11, 2001, came. I live downtown. I could see the horror outside my window. I ran out into the street when it happened, ran back home to decipher the horror on television, ran back out again, seeing dozens of dazed ash-covered survivors careening and stumbling in the streets—escaped from down there but escaping to where?—ran back home to make sense through television, sat there, paralyzed, my wife uptown at her office not able to get back home. Was she safe? Were we safe? If I stayed passively in front of the television, watching the event of the two explosions—and then the Pentagon—over and over, I would go crazy. Constant sirens. I could see the towers topple from my window. The air, heavy with smoke from the site, blew into our apartment. I shut the windows. It crept in. What elements did that smoke contain? It couldn't be flesh. (I bumped into a neighbor the second night who said, "Welcome to Auschwitz.") Was today our Cold Harbor? I didn't want to turn to stone. I had to do something. I remembered this play. I went into my workroom, turned on my computer, and, with all this in me and around me, turned off the television, pulled down the shades, and started work.

Three weeks later the air had cleared and I gave the finished play to James Houghton. I sent it to Donald Moffatt. Polly Holliday stopped by to have a cup of coffee. I gave her the play. "Can I be Mrs. Grant?" she asked. Michael Greif read the play and agreed to do it. Donald called and said he'd like to recommend a director he thought would be perfect: Michael Greif. William Sadler, a remarkable actor who bore a remarkable likeness to Samuel Clemens and was the same age as Clemens at the time of the play, had just moved back to New York after a long stint in Los Angeles. We were lucky to find him. Casting Adam Badeau, the villain of this play—and a villain he was—was a problem. Badeau, Grant's trusted aide, was anorexically thin, looking more like a vicious ink sketch than a person. We couldn't find a matching person. Tom McGowan, who is as portly as the real Badeau was thin, understood the essence of Badeau. We cast him. The Emperor and Empress were gifts from the gods. Cheryl Evans sang Adelina Patti. Gabriel Berry produced beautiful costumes with no apparent budget. David van Tiegham's underscoring linked the American and Japanese worlds within the play beautifully. The actress Marian Seldes sent me a copy of a Japanese print illustrating Grant's arrival in Japan. Her late husband, Garson Kanin, had saved the print for a play about Mrs. Grant that he had once considered writing, and it is used on the cover of this book.

When *A Few Stout Individuals* opened, the most common reaction I got was, "Is this true? This can't be true. How do you make this stuff up? It's true?" I imagined some of it—Harrison's involvement in the war, for example—but you bet it's all true, except for the tonic salesman, and I know even he existed.

Read the *Personal Memoirs*. It's up there with Melville and Hawthorne and Twain himself. I thank James Houghton and Signature for commissioning this play. I thank my wife for everything. And I thank that snooty stranger who asked me if I'd ever read Grant's *Personal Memoirs* in the first place.

A Few Stout Individuals was commissioned and produced by the
Signature Theater, New York, New York; James Houghton,
artistic director. It opened on May 12, 2002, with the following cast:

THE EMPEROR OF JAPAN	James Yaegashi
USG	Donald Moffatt
SAMUEL CLEMENS	William Sadler
MRS. G	Polly Holliday
ADAM BADEAU	Tom McGowan
THE EMPRESS OF JAPAN	Michi Barall
KARL GERHARDT	Umit Celebes
HARRISON	Charles Brown
NELL	Amy Hohn
FRED	T. J. Kenneally
BUCK	Mark Fish
THE FALSE CYRUS	Clark Middleton
ADELINA PATTI	Cheryl Evans

Director	Michael Greif
Stage Manager	Michael McGoff
Assistant Stage Manager	Marci Glotzer
Set Design	Allen Moyer
Costume Design	Gabriel Berry
Lighting Design	Jim Vermeulen
Original Music and Sound Design	David van Tieghem
Casting	Jerry Beaver Associates
Literary Manager	Beth Whitaker

ACT ONE: FEBRUARY 1885.
ACT TWO: THREE WEEKS LATER.
PLACE: 3 EAST SIXTY-SIXTH STREET, NEW YORK, NEW YORK.

ACT ONE

An extraordinary masked apparition appears: the EMPEROR OF JAPAN.

THE EMPEROR OF JAPAN   I am the emperor of Japan
> I am the throne of chrysanthemum
> I am the center of the disk that is the sun
> I am the horizon behind which the golden sun rises
> I give the sun to you each morning
> I take the sun back each night
> I am the moon who casts a cool light on the ocean
> > which I also am
> I am shadow
> I am light
> I am memory I am memory I am memory I am memory

A dark room, lit by a few hurricane lamps. USG, *sixty-three, but looking ancient, sits wrapped in blankets in a wheelchair, in pain, toothless, wasted, his voice a harsh fierce whisper.*

USG   But who am I?

THE EMPEROR OF JAPAN   I am the emperor of Japan
> I am the throne of chrysanthemum

USG   I know who you are. Who am I?

CLEMENS'S VOICE   Who am I? What is he saying?

THE EMPEROR OF JAPAN   Why did the South last so long?

USG   The south of what?

THE EMPEROR OF JAPAN   Why did the South fight? Were they all fighting for slavery?

USG   I don't know what you're talking about—

I

THE EMPEROR OF JAPAN They weren't all slaveholders. It's not why the South lost. How did they hold on so long? Why did it take you so long?

USG I didn't ask you here for this. I asked you—

THE EMPEROR OF JAPAN Why did you summon me?

USG I can't remember.

Other people are dimly visible in the room: SAMUEL CLEMENS, *a blustery man, fifty, red hair turning white.* MRS. G, *fifty-nine, terrified.* ADAM BADEAU, *fifties, very lame, pale, red hair.*

CLEMENS Give him something.

MRS. G Not time.

USG Hard.

CLEMENS Of course it's hard. The terror of the blank page—I understand that—

THE EMPEROR OF JAPAN How hard can it be? When in doubt, tell the truth.

USG You sound like my publisher—

THE EMPEROR OF JAPAN Who's your publisher?

USG I don't know.

CLEMENS Do you know? Do you know who I am?

THE EMPEROR OF JAPAN Do you know who I am?

USG The emperor of Japan.

CLEMENS Oh my God.

USG Why would you come visit me?

CLEMENS Because we have a contract.

2

THE EMPEROR OF JAPAN   Because you summoned me.

CLEMENS   For a book.

USG   Why would you obey me?

THE EMPEROR OF JAPAN   Because of who you are.

CLEMENS   Because of who you are.

USG   I know who you are. But me—me—me . . .

The EMPRESS OF JAPAN *appears. Like her husband, she is in her early twenties.*

THE EMPRESS OF JAPAN   He does not know who he is?

THE EMPEROR OF JAPAN   He calls me here—

CLEMENS   He doesn't know who he is. Help him.

THE EMPRESS OF JAPAN   Help him—

THE EMPEROR OF JAPAN   How? Give him some medicine.

CLEMENS   Give him some medicine.

MRS. G   He *is* a little bit under the weather.

CLEMENS   Under the weather? This man is under a cyclone, a tornado.

MRS. G   Sit up, Lyss, let me help you. Show what you can do.

THE EMPRESS OF JAPAN   Let me help you—

CLEMENS   Let me help you.

MRS. G   No! *I* help him. He's just having a day today. Some days he dictates ten thousand words. My pencil snaps, I can't keep up with him.

CLEMENS   That's what I want to hear. Pages. I've come to see pages.

MRS. G   Your cannabis pill—swallow—quickly—time for the cannabis.

CLEMENS   Take it—ease your pain.

USG   Who are you?

MRS. G   It's Mr. Clemens—

USG swallows with difficulty. He breathes.

USG   Clemens? Clemens?

The light turns golden on him. His voice is normal. He sits up. This transformation is only seen by the Emperor and Empress.

THE EMPEROR OF JAPAN (*Impressed*)   Samuel—is he also Mark Twain?

USG   Samuel Clemens? That's who he is!

CLEMENS   That's right, sir—Who did he think I was?

THE EMPEROR OF JAPAN   You know him!

USG   It appears I do.

THE EMPEROR OF JAPAN   He's publishing you? Why didn't you tell me! And he's promised you a fortune!

USG   Seventy percent of the profits. No author ever got seventy percent of the profits. I remember *that*.

THE EMPEROR OF JAPAN   —if there *are* any profits.

USG   Don't give me reality. I also remember I owe a man named Vanderbilt one hundred and fifty thousand dollars. Could it be we're losing this house?

MRS. G I can't believe they'd ever foreclose on this house—not after what you've done for them.

USG My children have moved back in. It appears we all need money. Clemens said he could sell a copy to every person who was in the war.

CLEMENS —to every man who was in the war—

USG —and I say, *what* war?

CLEMENS Is he serious?

BADEAU I'm afraid that—

MRS. G He's just having a bad day—

USG I must be somebody if he wants me to write my life and I must be somebody if I owe the richest man in America a fortune and I must be somebody if an emperor and his wife come to visit me. Should I kneel to you?

CLEMENS No, I should kneel to you.

THE EMPEROR OF JAPAN No no. You're my only equal. You're a great man.

USG That's what Clemens said three months ago when we started. A great man.

CLEMENS A great man.

THE EMPEROR OF JAPAN Did he give you advice on how to write?

USG "Stretch things all you want but just tell the truth."

THE EMPEROR OF JAPAN Very funny!

CLEMENS Exactly, sir—you remember. I'm very encouraged.

MRS. G   He's fine. He remembers.

THE EMPEROR OF JAPAN   "All you need in life is ignorance and confidence; then success is sure."

USG   "Familiarity breeds contempt—and children."

CLEMENS   You remember that? He's very charming—

THE EMPEROR OF JAPAN   "Reports of my death are vastly overrated."

USG   "Always do right. You will gratify some people and astonish the rest."

THE EMPEROR OF JAPAN & USG   "Repartee is something you remember twenty-four hours after you should have said it"—

CLEMENS   My only sorrow is that the world might not see what you can give. I don't want the world to forget you.

USG   You read Mark Twain?

THE EMPEROR OF JAPAN   I don't read. My readers read him to me.

USG   I don't think I ever read him. I like Victor Hugo. *Les Misérables*. That's my idea of a book.

THE EMPEROR OF JAPAN   A man being chased through sewers? I didn't identify with that.

CLEMENS   Does he want me to read Victor Hugo to him?

MRS. G   No, no, he read that on our way to Japan.

THE EMPEROR OF JAPAN   So that's Mark Twain—good advance?

USG   Biggest advance any author's ever got.

6

CLEMENS   Ten thousand dollars out of my own pocket.

THE EMPEROR OF JAPAN   Poor Japan. We have no one like him. Just as well. Wouldn't be easy for him to live there. I allow no books to be published.

USG   Why?

THE EMPEROR OF JAPAN   The people need no memories. I am enough.

USG   Mark Twain says if I write down my memories, besides being very rich I will also be immortal.

THE EMPEROR OF JAPAN   Wise Mark Twain.

USG   Happy Mark Twain.

THE EMPEROR OF JAPAN   But poor Mark Twain.

USG   Why poor?

THE EMPEROR OF JAPAN   He is not like you or me. He is only a writer. He is not an immortal.

USG   Not like *you*. The emperor of Japan. Immortal.

THE EMPEROR OF JAPAN   Not like *you*. President. General. Immortal.

USG   I was those things?

THE EMPEROR OF JAPAN   Why do you think I see you?

USG   Can you be a former immortal?

THE EMPEROR OF JAPAN   No. Immortal is immortal.

USG   Maybe in your country.

THE EMPEROR OF JAPAN   Make them remember you.

USG One of these people wants to kill me.

THE EMPEROR OF JAPAN Wants to kill you?

USG I'm not sure which one. What do they want from me?

THE EMPEROR OF JAPAN A great book.

USG But I have to write the damn thing.

THE EMPEROR OF JAPAN What's the problem?

USG I'm floating. They tell me to go into my memory . . .
but I don't even remember having a memory.

THE EMPEROR OF JAPAN Aside from that.

USG Oh, I'm dying.

The golden light fades on USG.

CLEMENS Oh God—

MRS. G No no no, he's just having a bad day.

USG (*To the Emperor*) I know why I called you. To save me!
To rescue me—you are memory.

CLEMENS Memory?

MRS. G He's famous for his memory. He looks at a map for
ten seconds, he knows the terrain better than any native!

CLEMENS How long has he been this way?

BADEAU What you see today began as one day a week. Then
two days a week. Then, like an ink blot, spread out over
the entire week. Like a fisherman, you sit through the storm
and wait it out. Like a teacup—

CLEMENS The pages, Mr. Badeau? Where are the new pages?

BADEAU   All this takes its toll.

CLEMENS   I left you with responsibility. You're my delegate—why didn't you let me know?

BADEAU   You're lollygagging around the country, promoting yourself giving readings of your new book, leaving explicit instructions not to disturb you.

CLEMENS   There are exceptions. I thought everything was swimming along, and now we're drowning.

BADEAU   If you're drowning in New York, you don't call a plumber who's somewhere between Canada and Texas.

USG   Who are you?

CLEMENS   Who am I?

THE EMPEROR OF JAPAN   You do know who I am.

USG   I know who you are. We are men with beautiful wives.

CLEMENS   Thank you.

THE EMPEROR OF JAPAN   Thank you.

THE EMPRESS OF JAPAN   Thank you.

MRS. G   Thank you.

CLEMENS   When did you meet my wife? She'll be so pleased. This is his charm—

MRS. G   All the wives are beautiful! Did you hear that? It's going to be all right. No problems—no problems at all—

Mrs. G kisses USG.

CLEMENS   But I came to see work—

9

BADEAU   The pages are right here. See—Vicksburg. The Wilderness.

CLEMENS   I saw those pages months ago. That began as the magazine article—

BADEAU   This big pile is West Point—this is Mexico—all new.

Clemens looks at the pages.

THE EMPEROR OF JAPAN   What is he reading?

USG   My new pages.

THE EMPEROR OF JAPAN   You haven't written anything.

USG   Oh, they do it for me.

THE EMPEROR OF JAPAN   Who wrote these pages?

CLEMENS   Who wrote these pages?

BADEAU   He did.

CLEMENS   This is not his voice—and this—"My roommate at West Point brought me home to Galena, Illinois, for the holidays. When I stepped off the train, Cupid must have had his arrow poised, for the first sight I saw was the girl of my dreams, wearing a red burgundy dress and attractive blue paisley shawl that complemented her eyes." The general did not write this.

MRS. G   It's exactly what he said. Didn't he?

BADEAU   I wasn't here that day.

CLEMENS   This is not his voice.

MRS. G   Are you calling the general a liar?! Or me?! He wrote this!

CLEMENS Even you can't admit that he wrote this or this—I'm saying he didn't write this—or this—or this. But he did write this: "My family is American, and has been for generations, in all its branches, direct and collateral." That's the way it begins and that's the tone in which it must continue. But this, "I never forgave the Bonapartes for their actions in Mexico. When I was in England and a guest at the tastefully decorated house of my great and heroic friend, Adam Badeau, I received an invitation to a party to meet the Prince Imperial, the son of Napoleon the Third. I declined the invitation. I said to my great friend, Adam Badeau, who had been injured in the war but never complained for one moment of his agony, that I was unwilling to show any courtesy to the son of . . ." He did not write this.

BADEAU You impugn him, not I.

CLEMENS It doesn't sound like him.

BADEAU This is what he sounds like now. All I do is take the dictation. If he compliments me, I accept it.

CLEMENS Then you must control his memory, guide his memory. When I was a pilot on the river, I learned to read its surface, to steer clear of the rocks, the eddies, the undercurrents. I hired you as my deputy because you've been with him so long—I thought you knew him.

BADEAU Alas. You're disappointed.

CLEMENS These new pages are unacceptable.

MRS. G We have the war. The war the war. This is the war. Well, most of the war.

CLEMENS Where is the presidency? I'm selling a two-volume book. We barely have enough usable material for one volume—no, not even for a long pamphlet. Sir? Can you talk? I have so many things to ask you.

THE EMPEROR OF JAPAN I have so many things to ask you.

USG Why?

EMPEROR OF JAPAN Because of who you are.

CLEMENS Because of who you are.

USG Who am I?

CLEMENS I'm very alarmed. You can smell the death on him.

MRS. G Don't say that word! He's had a little accident—

CLEMENS Make him comfortable.

MRS. G There's nothing to change him to. I've sent Harrison out to buy fresh underclothes—buy buy buy. The girl who did the laundry left us.

CLEMENS Left you?

MRS. G These servants come here so honored to be in the employ of the general—and then they forget their patriotism, that without him, there wouldn't be any America for them to work in and then they want money—yes, she left. The cook left. I can't do the laundry and also cook and tend the general. Thank God I still have Claudine. She does my hair—

BADEAU Your daughter is here from England.

MRS. G I cannot ask someone who is married to someone very close to the nobility to clean foul linen.

BADEAU This family—

MRS. G All right, I admit it; I forgot to do the laundry. Do you know who I am? And I am doing laundry. My story is the story to tell.

USG cries out, clutching his throat.

CLEMENS   Give him something!

MRS. G   Not time.

CLEMENS   His throat! Get him ice cream.

MRS. G   Ice cream! (*Calling*) Harrison!

Mrs. G crosses to the door and opens it. KARL GERHARDT, appears. He's thirty-two-years old, wearing an artists' smock over a business suit.

GERHARDT   Is it time?

CLEMENS   Not yet!

Gerhardt leaves. HARRISON appears.

MRS. G   Harrison, we want ice cream. Did you purchase the general's underclothes?

HARRISON   The deliveryman came back with me—cash on delivery.

MRS. G   They wouldn't charge?

HARRISON   No, ma'am.

MRS. G   How much is it?

Harrison gives her an invoice. She looks at it.

MRS. G   Mr. Clemens, do you have money for the general's underclothes? Or is that too greedy to ask?

Clemens gives her money.

CLEMENS (*To himself*)   How much do I need to get to the station?

HARRISON   Ma'am? Could I speak to you?

MRS. G   Later. Give the deliveryman this amount, and then with the change go over to Madison Avenue for a pint of that chocolate ice cream and a pint of—

HARRISON   Ma'am, meaning no disrespect, it's not enough and they will extend us no more credit—

MRS. G   Then find a sweetshop on Lexington Avenue.

HARRISON   There is no ice cream on Lexington Avenue.

MRS. G   Do you have money for ice cream?

Clemens gives her money.

CLEMENS   (*To us*)   Do I have enough to get to Philadelphia?

HARRISON   May I speak to you?

MRS. G   You can see we are busy with the general's publisher. Our first line of duty is to freshen the general up—

Harrison and Mrs. G push USG out of the room.

USG   Don't leave me!

CLEMENS   We're here.

THE EMPEROR OF JAPAN   We're here.

The Emperor and Empress of Japan follow. Clemens throws up his hands.

CLEMENS   It all seemed so easy. Hire the general to write his memoirs. Sell a copy to every veteran. What could go wrong?

Badeau enters, closing the door behind him.

BADEAU   Contrary to appearances, we have everything under control.

CLEMENS   Control? Open your eyes in this dark airless room. Have I made a mistake in hiring you as my delegate? You promised me three months ago you'd have his story wrapped up by now and ready for the printers. I'm blithely selling unwritten copies around the country ready for delivery on Memorial Day. This is the vastest publishing project ever conceived. I've slaughtered forests of trees to make paper for six hundred thousand volumes. Drained oceans of ink to print the book. Hired a score of pressmen to be available for printing the monster. Hired twenty printing presses to churn the thing out! Like something shameless P. T. Barnum would stoop to, I've enlisted thousands of old veterans to take their uniforms out of mothballs and get out there and start selling his book, which they are doing. I've written them a script. (*To us*) "Is there a veteran in the house? If you love your country, it is your duty to buy a copy of the general's memoirs." And people are buying.

BADEAU   We never see any money.

CLEMENS   There are thousands of dollars in escrow. You'll get your ten thousand dollars when you deliver the pages. Finish the book and the money will shower down on all of us in torrents. I want to see work.

Mrs. G opens the door, pushing in USG.

MRS. G   Fresh as a daisy!

USG   Where are you?

CLEMENS   Right here.

The Emperor and Empress of Japan appear.

THE EMPEROR & EMPRESS OF JAPAN   Right here.

Gerhardt peers in.

GERHARDT   Is it time?

CLEMENS   Not yet.

The door closes.

MRS. G   He's all yours, shiny and raring to go!

BADEAU   Let us recollect.

USG   Recollect what?

THE EMPEROR OF JAPAN   Your life—

USG   My life? What life?

CLEMENS   What life!

BADEAU   I'm sorry.

MRS. G   The day of the dog show, the dog always rolls over. It's human nature—

CLEMENS   This morning saw me railroading down from Quebec watching the world go by. Buttering toast. Reading in the paper how the general was in his New York City home happily writing his memoirs. How well sales were going. I felt so happy. I counted my money. I counted his money. I counted our money. I saw our dollars piling high. Was it all a dream?

BADEAU   I gave that to the press to create interest in the book.

CLEMENS And I still believe what I read in the papers. I get here and what do I see? Devastation. I come in this beautiful house on Central Park that three months ago was filled with treasures—gifts from around the world—elephant tusks of ivory—swords—uniforms—trophies made of gold—flags. The house is stripped bare.

MRS. G Everything sent to Mr. Vanderbilt to honor a debt. Lyss didn't steal that money from him, no matter what people say.

CLEMENS Have they moved out? I come up these stairs today and see the general like a Madame Tussaud wax figure out of the Chamber of Horrors. Are you sure this is the same vibrant man I saw three and a half months ago when we started this project? Tell me—how could everything fall apart? Where is the nurse?

BADEAU She let her go. I had nothing to do with that—

MRS. G I caught her writing her own memoir, called "Escorting the General into Eternity." This man is hardly approaching eternity and *his* will be the only memoir written in this house—although I'd like to talk to you about publishing my recollections of life as a companion volume—

CLEMENS We'll get his memoirs published first, then talk about yours.

MRS. G My memories are his memories. Sit up, my dear.

CLEMENS (*To Badeau*) Don't tell me I've made a mistake with you—have I?

BADEAU You have no right to blame me or be angry at me.

USG Pain.

CLEMENS   Give him something.

MRS. G   Not time.

CLEMENS   Ease his pain.

MRS. G   I have to have the right balance—

CLEMENS   Find it.

MRS. G   I thought I had the right balance—you and your buzz-saw voice have thrown him off balance, me off kilter. It's a very delicate regimen—cannabis—morphine— cocaine—he has to come off one before he goes on the other. He can't get so acclimated to the drugs they don't do any good—I can't keep increasing the doses—the morphine has to wear off before I swab his throat with the cocaine. Hold on, my Victor—hold on.

CLEMENS   I'm dizzy. This airless room. Why does she call him Victor?

MRS. G   Oh, a bit of brandy can't hurt. Would you like some brandy my Lyssy? The bottle's empty. How could the bottle be empty? (*Calls*) Harrison! Harrison!

Harrison enters, dragging a sack of mail. Gerhardt, ever hopeful, waves. Clemens shuts the door on him.

MRS. G   Bring another bottle of brandy.

HARRISON   The brandy's all gone.

BADEAU   Put the mail over here.

MRS. G   We just bought a case. Give the mail to me.

HARRISON   I have instructions.

Harrison sets the mail sack by Badeau. NELL enters. She is thirty-years old, and has a very upper-class British accent.

NELL Is there a letter for me?

BADEAU I'll go through the mail.

NELL My husband hasn't written. There's something very wrong with the American postal system.

BADEAU I'll give you yours when I find it.

CLEMENS *(To Nell)* Mrs. Sartoris, I believe. We haven't met. I'm—

NELL Are we prisoners here?

CLEMENS Are you having a pleasant stay—

MRS. G This is my house. This is my mail.

CLEMENS The general's in pain.

MRS. G Bring him brandy. That's my daughter. Lives in England. Married to someone very close to the nobility.

NELL Oh, Mother!

HARRISON The brandy's all gone.

MRS. G Then go buy another case of brandy.

HARRISON They want money.

MRS. G Charge it.

HARRISON They want money.

MRS. G Do they know who it's for?

HARRISON They know who it's for.

MRS. G Then just get one bottle.

HARRISON   They want money.

Mrs. G looks through her purse.

MRS. G   These people want money. If it wasn't for this man, they wouldn't even be living in America. They'd be living in a collection of desolate little principalities. The Kingdom of Kentucky. The Duchy of Dakota. The Monarchy of Manhattan. No gratitude anywhere. I don't have—

NELL   All I have are pound notes. And not many of those—

MRS. G   Mr. Badeau?

BADEAU   Don't look at me. I'm the hired help.

MRS. G (*To Clemens*)   May I speak to you privately? This man comes in this house to help my husband write a book and he takes over. I'm so glad you're here. It is a reign of terror here. We are prisoners here. Help me.

Clemens gives Harrison money.

CLEMENS   Do I have enough to get to Philadelphia and then to the lecture hall? Get one bottle.

HARRISON (*To Mrs. G*)   May I speak to you?

MRS. G   Not now—can't you see we are with the general's publisher?

Harrison goes. Gerhardt looks in.

GERHARDT   Is it time?

CLEMENS   Not yet.

The door closes.

NELL   My husband may have written. I have to have some contact with the outside world. In spite of my being immured here, I've learned that Mrs. Vanderbilt is having a gala tonight for the marchioness of Salisbury.

BADEAU I know her.

NELL Oh, Mother! The marchioness's gardens at Hatfield are one of the wonders of the world.

CLEMENS Then let her go home and prune them. We are trying to work—

NELL And she's in New York! I've always dreamed of gaining admittance to the very garden where the young Elizabeth learned she would be queen of England—to bask in the very flower-filled spot where the Elizabethan Age began. That's where I belong. To achieve entry to that garden of splendid memory! My husband wouldn't laugh at America if I told him 'twas in America I finally met the marchioness of Salisbury.

BADEAU I met her.

MRS. G Go to it, dear.

NELL We're not invited, Mother—to the Vanderbilts' or anywhere—since Father had his shady financial dealings.

USG Pay the debt—pay the debt—

NELL Father? Why did you have to bilk Mr. Vanderbilt?

MRS. G Your father did not! He was a victim as much as—

NELL Once I could come to New York and hold my head up high in the social swim. Sift through my cornucopia of gala invitations. What did Mr. Poe's raven say? "Nevermore." Why did Father have to take money from the man who controls the very social fabric of this city?

Nell goes.

MRS. G My daughter's husband—this close to the royal family—

Mrs. G goes. Gerhardt peers in.

GERHARDT Is it—

CLEMENS Not yet!

Clemens closes the door. Badeau opens mail.

BADEAU This mail. Typical day. "Thief." "You ruined me." "Where's my money?" "Foreclosure." "Pay or else." That's why I go through the mail first. I remove all the letters of rage and anguish. "You ruined me and you're still living on Fifth Avenue."

CLEMENS Don't let him hear this. Don't rub it in.

BADEAU Let him hear it. Perhaps it'll prod him to write. I know he's innocent. Every day I urge him to recover. Not to let him think his immense achievements have been crushed by the outrageous falsity and guile of his business partner, Ferdinand Ward, that monster in craft who selected him, the people's hero, as his victim and decoy. I tell the general to use this book not simply to tell his life, but to explain his current circumstances and redeem himself in the eyes of the world.

THE EMPEROR OF JAPAN If you are in shame, you should kill yourself.

USG I am not going to commit suicide.

CLEMENS Suicide! No.

USG Don't worry.

CLEMENS He hears. He speaks.

THE EMPEROR OF JAPAN   It is a very noble act.

BADEAU   He hears. He speaks. When that wife's out of the room, he can speak. That mynah bird is gone. Perhaps we can get to work.

CLEMENS   How do you begin?

BADEAU   The open sesame is "Let us recollect."

CLEMENS   Let us recollect. Tell me about the war.

THE EMPEROR OF JAPAN   Tell me about the war.

USG   War?

CLEMENS   The presidency—

USG   President of what? Lost . . . lost . . .

CLEMENS   You don't lose a war. You don't lose a presidency.

THE EMPEROR OF JAPAN   You don't lose a war—you don't lose a presidency—

CLEMENS   You may forget where you put your eyeglasses or your wallet (*Mrs. G enters*) but you don't lose a war—what are you telling me?!

THE EMPEROR OF JAPAN   What are you telling me?

BADEAU   I have a recently published book that will explain and perhaps soothe any worries you might—

CLEMENS   *Diseases of Memory?*

BADEAU   *Diseases of Memory* by a brilliant French physician, Ribot. I've met him.

MRS. G   It's not any scientific hoo-ha about his memory. He's famous for his memory. He's hungry. He can't eat anything

23

but beef bouillon or calf's-foot jelly. That's not enough to hold body and soul together. He needs a shave. Harrison! Harrison! I've forgotten he's gone. We all forget. It's not a disease.

BADEAU   This marvelous bit of modern science helps me understand memory in a way that allows me to devise a strategy. Memory is nothing mysterious. Memory is merely an organic bodily function, like digestion or perspiration. "The brain is like a laboratory full of movement, where thousands of occupations are going on at once. Not being subject to restrictions of time, operating . . . only in space, it may act in several directions at the same moment. Consciousness is the narrow gate through which a very small part of all this work is able to reach us . . . The basis of memory is nutrition."

CLEMENS   Nutrition?

MRS. G   Calf's-foot jelly.

BADEAU   There's nothing transcendent about memory. It's a bodily function. Find the proper nutrition, the proper stimulus, and you will unlock the narrow gate of the unconscious.

CLEMENS   It's all in the proper stimulant?

BADEAU   I am searching for the proper *stimulus* to open that narrow keyhole of the conscious and let the flood of unconscious memory flow out. I show him photographs. I've even brought in gunpowder for him to smell. I have him in his uniform. Finding the proper stimulus. That's my main task. There's no reason to worry.

CLEMENS   Have you brought any of his fellow officers here? They could talk about old times—

24

MRS. G We brought in General Sherman—

BADEAU He only talked about his own memoirs that he's writing. No help at all.

MRS. G Then we brought in General Lew Wallace. That was a disaster. He only wanted to talk about *Ben-Hur*.

USG (*Violently*) No *Ben-Hur*!

MRS. G No *Ben-Hur*. That a subordinate like Wallace could write a financial triumph like *Ben-Hur*. How do you think that makes Lyss feel—

CLEMENS (*Aside*) Maybe that's what I should write. Ancient Rome. The Colosseum. Gladiators. Chariot races—

BADEAU Bringing in other soldiers hasn't worked.

MRS. G I'm the proper stimulus. He responds only to me—

CLEMENS I don't want any book explaining memory to me. I have invested a fortune in publishing the memoirs of the century. And he can't remember? I like things to be funny but this goes too far.

BADEAU We're at the end of the war. Tell about signing the armistice. Is the legend of the apple tree correct? It's all about finding the proper stimulus.

CLEMENS You keep saying that.

Badeau takes out photographs.

BADEAU See this courthouse? That's you. Do you recognize you? That's General Lee. Do you recognize him? This is stimulus.

CLEMENS You're at Appomattox—good good.

MRS. G Oh, what a day that was! I wore a blue brocaded dress with a gray taffeta sash to commemorate both sides that were signing the surrender.

CLEMENS Where is Fort Sumter? Where is the beginning of the war?

BADEAU We haven't got there yet. Sir, look at these photographs.

CLEMENS Then how can you write the solution to the war if you lack the initial insult that started the war?

BADEAU We do not work within the confines of chronology. His mind wanders here—

CLEMENS Confines?

BADEAU It's a story. You're telling our reader a story. Don't you control him? Tell me, sir. Alleviate my fears—sir? Where were you when the war began?

USG Japan? Blue islands. Green sea.

CLEMENS We're not in Japan. You're in New York City on Sixty-sixth Street and Fifth Avenue. Central Park is right there—

MRS. G He's in Japan because it's the happiest we ever were. Is Japan in the book? That's what people want to read about. Not all this war. We sailed there—

USG I remember that.

MRS. G Is it only six years ago we were in Japan? We met the emperor. What a nice young man—

USG They told us you were a god and it is an honor simply to behold you.

MRS. G We stepped into the reception room in the palace. The emperor—whom we were told was a god and it was an honor simply to behold him—appeared.

USG You appeared.

THE EMPEROR OF JAPAN I appeared. My wife by my side.

THE EMPRESS OF JAPAN I bowed.

USG I bowed.

THE EMPEROR OF JAPAN I bowed.

MRS. G He bowed to us, which was an event in itself, and then for the first time in the history of Japan, the emperor, who is also called the mikado, stepped forward of his own accord and shook Lyss's hand.

THE EMPEROR OF JAPAN I hadn't planned. I did it. I was breathless meeting you—

THE EMPRESS OF JAPAN He was so overcome meeting you.

THE EMPEROR OF JAPAN A soldier—a man who had lived!

USG I'm a soldier?

THE EMPEROR OF JAPAN The greatest soldier. What is it like to lead an army?

MRS. G He touched a mere mortal's hand. And then spoke to him! With admiration!

THE EMPEROR OF JAPAN It was a scandal!

MRS. G A revolutionary act comparable to the French Revolution, the American Revolution!

THE EMPRESS OF JAPAN No emperor had ever touched a commoner.

27

MRS. G   The emperor had never touched a commoner, although there is nothing common about my Lyss.

THE EMPEROR OF JAPAN   I decreed that all of Japan must pay you homage. Even though they didn't know who you were, I did. My readers keep me up on all aspects of the world. When I found out you were coming to Japan, I was determined to meet you.

MRS. G   We were the idols of Japan. A play written about us. The story of your life.

THE EMPEROR OF JAPAN   I had a hand in the writing of that play!

MRS. G   Remember, Lyss? Sailing into Yokohama, traveling to Tokyo. All along the way, silent crowds lining the roads waiting to see us, the American general, the American president. All silent. Thousands of silent people.

USG   Japan . . .

CLEMENS   Japan.

MRS. G   That's the way they cheer in Japan. American cheers are Japanese silences. The more excited the Japanese are, the quieter the Japanese are. To each his own. We visited the emperor of Japan and his wife. He came forward, not wearing a kimono but wearing some sort of army uniform, and said for the world to hear that he and Lyss were the two most powerful men in the world.

THE EMPEROR OF JAPAN   The two most powerful men in the world.

USG   The two most powerful men in the world.

MRS. G   All the aides gasped. But it was true. At the time. His wife was so pretty. Dressed in a plain white dress. What a night that was! Fireworks! A man in a top hat all in rockets! Was it Lincoln? Was it Lyss? Food! Fifty courses! The menu was as thick as a novel by Victor Hugo. Looking back, probably the most beautiful night ever. That's the reason for memory—to retrospect beauty. Let him remember Japan.

CLEMENS Unfortunately it's not what I'm selling.

MRS. G If he's in Japan let him stay there. I hope if I ever get to this state I'll have a Japan to escape to.

CLEMENS I'm very happy for his current state of geography, but we have a contract that calls for him not to be in Japan but to be in New York City working. General, sit up. Please.

USG Can't.

USG gasps. FRED, *thirties, opens the door.*

FRED Can I do anything for anyone?

CLEMENS Oh, your son. How nice to see—

USG My son!

USG rails.

FRED Not that son—the other son—the good son—it's Fred—it's not Buck—it's Fred—see—Little Dog—

USG strokes Fred's face.

USG Good little dog.

FRED Can I do anything? I have my chronologies. I have records of the war. I have names.

BADEAU We're quite fine, thank you.

FRED I'm of value. I'm more than eager to help.

CLEMENS Thank you for offering—

MRS. G Let me swab his poor gums with cocaine.

FRED I lost all my money in Father's catastrophe. I have to live here. While my wife and children are in the country with her family.

MRS. G (*To USG*) Open up.

FRED I'm trying to get some money together to start again— If you hear of anything—

BADEAU & CLEMENS Yes yes.

MRS. G That's better.

FRED I'd like to be of service.

BADEAU We'll call you.

Fred goes. Gerhardt peers in.

GERHARDT Is it time?

CLEMENS Not yet.

The door closes. Golden light on USG.

THE EMPEROR OF JAPAN You seem worried—

USG Understatement. I live on the brink of an abyss. My son cost me a million dollars.

THE EMPEROR OF JAPAN That son?

USG Another son.

MRS. G We had a million dollars one day and the next day— feathers.

USG A million dollars . . .

CLEMENS   You remember that.

THE EMPEROR OF JAPAN   You remember that.

MRS. G   I use the proper stimulus—my love.

BADEAU   And cocaine.

USG   That's all I remember—that I was a very rich man. Until my son's partner bamboozled the money out of us. My son's business partner is up the river in Sing Sing.

THE EMPEROR OF JAPAN   Sing Sing—such a beautiful name—

USG   Well, he was my business partner too. The firm of Grant and Ward. At least my son's not in Sing Sing. At least I'm not in Sing Sing—yet. Do you have sons?

CLEMENS   I had a son—who died—I think of him every day. Why is he asking about my son?

THE EMPEROR OF JAPAN   Sons? Hundreds of them.

USG   Poor man—watch out—

THE EMPEROR OF JAPAN   You had a million dollars?

USG   Which Buck lost.

THE EMPEROR OF JAPAN   Is that a lot?

USG   Yes! Don't you know about money?

THE EMPEROR OF JAPAN   No. In my country I *am* money.

USG   In my country I'm not. I have to pay Mr. Vanderbilt back the hundred and fifty thousand dollars he gave me to float the firm. "Write your memoirs. I'll publish them. We'll all make a fortune." That's what this man said. He showed up right after the financial disaster.

31

MRS. G Mr. Vanderbilt doesn't need to be paid back.

USG I gave my word.

CLEMENS Sir, you have the rarest memory of our century—

THE EMPEROR OF JAPAN The rarest memory of our century—

THE EMPRESS OF JAPAN The rarest memory of eternity—

CLEMENS You have been at the center of the greatest conflict of this century.

THE EMPEROR OF JAPAN You have been at the center of the greatest conflict of this century.

CLEMENS And your memory is a gold mine. What did Emerson say—"What is history? No more than the biographies of a few stout individuals." Your life is the story of our life. You are currently destitute. Your memory is your greatest asset.

USG My memory . . .

CLEMENS What separates us from the beasts is memory, but the paradox is that memory separates us, each from the other. Until we share that memory, we are truly alone. That is the purpose of art, of history, of love. If you share your unique memory with the world, you will give America its memory. The war will be truly over. We will finally become a nation with one memory—and with that memory, we will never fight a war again. Not since Julius Caesar wrote *The Gallic Wars* has a military hero begun to write a greater military history than you, you have to finish it.

BADEAU Julius Caesar, very overrated.

Golden light fades on USG.

CLEMENS If Wellington had written about Waterloo—

USG (*Rage*) No Wellington!

CLEMENS Certainly he has no brief against Wellington—

MRS. G Well, he may not. But I do. When we were in England, we went to dinner with the second duke of Wellington at his house—

BADEAU Apsley House.

MRS. G Apsley House—a magnificent house that the British government gave to his father, the first duke of Wellington, along with wealth and a title. And for what? For winning one battle—all right, it *was* Waterloo—a great *victory*—but it was one battle. It's not four years of a man's life. It's not pulling a country together. It's not rescuing a nation that was in danger of vanishing—and here we are on the brink of poverty. Mr. Clemens, is there any money?

CLEMENS You must believe me.

MRS. G Lyss, you have to write the book. It's our only hope. I'm going to get you some nourishment. Some marrow pudding. Keep your strength up, my warrior, my Victor. That's the only nutrition you need.

USG in pain.

CLEMENS Give him something.

MRS. G Not time.

CLEMENS Not time not time. You're like Big Ben in reverse. I can't bear to see him like this—give him something—no matter what time it is.

Mrs. G goes to a table with medical bottles on it.

MRS. G The morphine, the cannabis, the hydrochlorate of cocaine—thank God we're living today. The bottle's empty. Where is the other bottle of cocaine? There was another bottle. Where has it gone? Fred?!

Mrs. G opens the door.

MRS. G Fred!

Gerhardt peers in.

GERHARDT Is it time?

CLEMENS No!

Fred comes in and closes the door.

MRS. G Fred! The cocaine is gone.

FRED You're not suggesting that I—

MRS. G I'm just asking you—and the morphine! They were full just—when did we refill them?

FRED Last week—weeks ago—don't ask me—I have no idea.

MRS. G Just tell me the truth!

FRED I find it so interesting that you don't ask Nell!

MRS. G Nell would never. She is married to someone very close to the nobility.

FRED What about you? You sound absolutely guilty.

BADEAU I think she's been dipping into the general's supply—

MRS. G What are you saying? That I—! Send Claudine in here—it's that cleaning girl—always cleaning so quickly— Claudine! Claudine?

FRED   Mr. Badeau fired her.

MRS. G   Without telling me?

BADEAU   I fired her this morning. She was rude to me. She wanted her salary. I told her I had nothing to pay her with. She left.

MRS. G   Who will take care of me? Look at my cuffs.

FRED   She must have taken the cocaine—the morphine—not I.

CLEMENS   No one's accusing you.

MRS. G   Get Harrison—

Mrs. G opens the door. Gerhardt waves in.

FRED   Harrison?

GERHARDT   May I come in?

CLEMENS   Not yet—

MRS. G   Harrison!

Harrison comes in with the brandy. Light. USG recoils. The door closes.

MRS. G   Harrison—do you know anything about the missing contents of this bottle or this bottle?

HARRISON   No, ma'am. I have the brandy.

MRS. G   We're supposed to believe that—

HARRISON   I know nothing about the contents of that bottle. I wash the general. I put him to bed. I wake him. I've done that twenty years. Shall I open the brandy?

Mrs. G takes the brandy.

MRS. G Go to the apothecary and buy this much cocaine.

HARRISON They won't let me charge any more.

MRS. G The general needs it for pain.

HARRISON The pharmacy wants to be paid.

USG Pain—pain . . .

MRS. G Did you tell them who it is for?

HARRISON They know who it's for. They want to be paid.

MRS. G Then go to another pharmacy—

HARRISON I've been to them all. They want money.

MRS. G Bring the chemist here. Let him see what cruelty he is inflicting on the general. Don't they care? Without this man, they wouldn't be living in America. They'd be living in the Monarchy of Manhattan—

CLEMENS Here's money—get it—

Clemens gives Harrison money.

HARRISON May I speak to you?

MRS. G Oh. All right.

Harrison and Mrs. G go in a corner. Clemens checks his wallet.

CLEMENS (*To us*) Do I have enough to get to the station? Do I have enough to buy a ticket to Philadelphia? I'm a fool. I laugh at my brother for trying to invent a perpetual motion machine to make his fortune. How am I any different? I have invested a fortune in a typesetting machine I'm trying to develop. I have invested a substantial amount of my fortune in developing a photo album with self-sticking paper. I'm always looking for my fortune. Sometimes I'll even write a book. My last two have been failures. I write a new book. I can't put my hopes on that. And then this windfall comes into my lap. The great man needs money and is willing to write his memoirs. I'll publish the great man's memoirs. Make *my* fortune, *his* fortune. I'll never have to write again. Wait for the magic to arrive in my hands. I'll publish it on Memorial Day, the twentieth anniversary of the end of the war. So simple—so simple— what could go wrong?

MRS. G (*Loud to Harrison*) Do you have any doubt you'll be paid? I can't believe the impudence after what this man has done for you. This man was your general—you veterans should work for nothing.

HARRISON Wait till you have to feed a family.

MRS. G I do have to feed a family. The government's flinging money away to you veterans. Aren't you getting this new pension? We can't get a pension.

USG (*Railing*) Pension? Pension!

MRS. G Don't you think this breaks his heart? That he who led the forces to *victory* does not qualify for a pension—

USG Pension?

CLEMENS He doesn't get a pension?

BADEAU He had to resign from the army to become president. He's ineligible.

CLEMENS Ineligible? This man?

MRS. G No money. No money at all. Do you have a pension?

HARRISON The pension gives me eight dollars a month.

MRS. G Call that your salary from him. Eight dollars a month would at least buy ice cream. More than we have. Mr. Clemens, do you get a pension?

CLEMENS No, I was on the other side and I deserted.

BADEAU I wouldn't boast.

CLEMENS I'm not.

HARRISON Shall I bring the ice cream?

MRS. G Leave it in the icebox.

HARRISON It should be eaten swiftly, ma'am. There's no ice.

MRS. G Then go buy some!

Harrison holds out his hand. Clemens gives him money. Harrison leaves.

GERHARDT Is it time?

CLEMENS Not yet.

Clemens slams the door.

MRS. G This valet. Those people should have such pride in serving us. Loyal people? All they want is money. Lyss, let us retrospect.

CLEMENS Give him his brandy.

MRS. G Oh yes, give you your brandy.

CLEMENS Do you need a glass?

MRS. G He can't drink it. All fluid is like liquid fire. I take the needle and—and I'd like to put it in *my* arm to quiet me. Get *my* hand to stop shaking. I inject the brandy directly into his bloodstream.

Mrs. G injects USG. Drums play. Golden light.

USG Explosion
Fire in the veins
Veins Vesuvius
Japan Japanese Vesuvius
Fujiyama
Peerless mount
Brandy puts out Fujiyama
Am I safe?
Are you there? Hello? Are you there?

The Emperor appears.

THE EMPEROR OF JAPAN I am the emperor of Japan
I am the throne of chrysanthemum
I am the center of the disk that is the sun
I've been waiting for you.

USG I've been waiting for you.

THE EMPEROR OF JAPAN & USG Moon and memory
Reflect on the trembling lake
Day forgets the moon

EMPRESS OF JAPAN That's a haiku.

USG collapses. The lights return to normal.

CLEMENS What is wrong?

BADEAU It's a reaction to the drugs and the brandy. Finding the proper balance—I'm not worried—

CLEMENS Not worried!

MRS. G It all started at our villa in New Jersey last summer. I gave Lyss a plate of delicious peaches, of which he is very partial. He bit into one, then started up. "Something has

39

stung me from that peach!" He hurled that peach out the window. I gave him water. He rinsed his throat again and again. He said water hurt him like liquid fire. But he kept on . . . That was the beginning of his throat trouble. That damned insect bite. A dragonfly. A wasp.

BADEAU Can we get to work? Sir? Wake up!

MRS. G Let him rest—

CLEMENS (*To Badeau*) You look so calm.

BADEAU I'm not worried. I'll find the proper stimulus—

CLEMENS Not worried!

MRS. G Plus he's had trouble with his teeth. You know how it destroys you when you have trouble with your teeth. The dentist who is also a butcher removed four teeth, leaving his gums infected. He also took a streetcar to the dentist and caught a cold. Take that into account.

CLEMENS You have your own carriage and coachman—

MRS. G That was the first luxury to go.

CLEMENS Why isn't he taking a cab?

MRS. G There's no money for cabs—

CLEMENS I gave you ten thousand dollars precisely to care for him—

BADEAU Tell your publisher why it can't be returned.

MRS. G It's been spent.

CLEMENS On what?

MRS. G My children have families.

CLEMENS The money was for him!

BADEAU The missus gave her daughter money to send to her husband in England. That's why she's waiting to hear so urgently from him. The daughter only came to America to get more money.

MRS. G That's not true! Nell and Algernon have an estate in Southampton, England.

BADEAU "Warsash"!

MRS. G The world flocks to "Warsash." Nobility! Royalty! Princes of the realm!

BADEAU It's the old story. When he married her, he thought she had money. When she married him, she thought he had money.

CLEMENS Does no one in the world have money?

BADEAU There's no money for brandy, for medicine, for food. And even if we did want him to go to hospital, we'd lose control over him. There's no book if he goes to hospital.

CLEMENS A sanatorium.

BADEAU They don't have the money for sanatoria.

CLEMENS I gave you ten thousand dollars. The biggest advance any author has ever received. Don't tell me it's gone.

MRS. G We have normal expenses.

BADEAU He repaid some of the people who lost their money. He still owes Vanderbilt.

CLEMENS   Sell something. This house was filled with trophies from around the world—things of gold.

THE EMPEROR OF JAPAN   I gave you a fan.

USG   The Japanese fan.

MRS. G   We sent them all to Mr. Vanderbilt.

THE EMPEROR OF JAPAN   You gave my fan away!

CLEMENS   Why? He's the richest man in America!

THE EMPEROR OF JAPAN   That fan depicted in gold threads the way I created the earth and sun and moon—

USG   Gave it away.

THE EMPEROR OF JAPAN   Gave it away!

THE EMPRESS OF JAPAN   You gave that fan away!

MRS. G   In some way of reducing the debt of a hundred and fifty thousand dollars.

THE EMPEROR OF JAPAN   I have heard about insults. I have never experienced an insult. It is most unpleasant.

THE EMPRESS OF JAPAN   Calm down—

USG   Don't go!

THE EMPRESS OF JAPAN   Have some pity on the man.

THE EMPEROR OF JAPAN   He gave away something I gave only to him.

BADEAU   Plus bills for housekeeping, dressmaking, food, wine, the staff, the cooks, the laundresses, the coachman, the horses, the carriage. Ten thousand dollars goes very quickly.

USG Don't leave.

THE EMPEROR OF JAPAN I regret that I ever met you.

The Emperor of Japan vanishes.

USG No!

MRS. G We have a standard to maintain. People look up to us—

THE EMPRESS OF JAPAN I apologize for my husband. No one has ever crossed him before. But you shouldn't have given away that fan!

The Empress of Japan vanishes.

BADEAU About my money—

CLEMENS You'll get your ten thousand when you deliver the book. Stand up, sir. Tell me there's nothing wrong with his walking. He bragged that he walks everywhere in New York. Three months ago, we walked around the city talking of this book. You don't collapse this quickly—

MRS. G Last Christmas, he went out on the frozen street to give the coachman a Christmas present. An envelope full of too much money. That's where your ten thousand dollars went. Christmas bonuses to coachmen. And then he slipped.

CLEMENS He can't walk?

BADEAU He fell on the ice.

MRS. G And revived an old war injury.

BADEAU He dislocated his hip.

CLEMENS Take him to the hospital.

BADEAU We did. They sent him back. Manage his pain. That's all—

MRS. G He's had a string of bad luck.

USG Bad luck—

CLEMENS This is bigger than bad luck. He should be in a hospital.

USG No hosp—no hosp—

MRS. G I don't want him in a hospital. I tended him on the battlefield, I tended him in the White House. I don't give up control over my Victor! I can care for him—oh my Victor—you're safe—you're home.

Mrs. G embraces USG. Badeau takes Clemens aside.

CLEMENS Who is Victor?

BADEAU I have a proposition I'd like to make you regarding the ownership of the general's memoirs.

CLEMENS The general owns his memories.

BADEAU I'm afraid that lawsuits are about to start. People are aware that if the book is the success you brag it will be, this fortune you promise will be garnished by investors who lost all their money in the general's Wall Street debacle.

CLEMENS And you're suggesting—

BADEAU I have a paper here—assigning the copyright to— to me.

CLEMENS To you.

BADEAU The name is blank. I'd assumed you would put in my name as someone who cannot be sued if I owned the copyright on the memoirs—

CLEMENS What about the family?

BADEAU Trust this family with anything to do with security? They'd sell off the copyright in a moment.

CLEMENS What about me?

BADEAU It would be unseemly for the publisher to own the book outright. I could imagine all kinds of suspicion falling on you—as though you were exploiting the man who's been exploited enough—

CLEMENS Let me see the paper.

BADEAU I'm the logical choice.

USG Is that why he wants to kill me?

CLEMENS We don't have to decide this right now.

BADEAU When do you decide? When the book is in the stores?

CLEMENS Mr. Badeau, when will there be a book?

BADEAU If I am given a freer rein, I can produce a book—

CLEMENS That *you* would write?

BADEAU I know the way he thinks, I know the way he should be seen. Don't you want the general at his best? If you have regard for him, for his place in history—

The door opens. Fred comes in, urgently. Gerhardt peers in.

FRED Mr. Badeau?

GERHARDT Is it time?

CLEMENS Not yet.

45

The door closes.

FRED Mr. Badeau—there's someone for you at the front door—very important—a publisher! And Mother! Go! There's a fire in the kitchen!

USG Fire? Fire?

MRS. G When do the boils and locusts begin?

Badeau rushes out. Mrs. G goes. Fred bolts the door and advances on Clemens.

FRED There's no fire. There's no fire. There's no publisher.

CLEMENS (*Backing away*) I wish you'd keep those doors unlocked.

FRED Sir, you should be told the truth.

CLEMENS All I see is truth. I'm surrounded by truth. I'm tripping over truth—so what is the truth telling me now?

FRED *Epithelial.*

CLEMENS What is that word?

FRED *Epithelial* is a polite word for the worst word.

CLEMENS Loss of memory? Loss of a fortune? Loss of—?

FRED Life. My father's dying.

CLEMENS Dying?

FRED When you saw my father three months ago, he was in remission.

CLEMENS What are you saying?

FRED The man is dying. It's important you know that! Look at Dr. Douglas's report.

46

Clemens takes the pages.

CLEMENS The *epithelium?*—what is—

FRED *Epi*—"upon"—"*epithelium:* the cell tissue that invests the outer surface of the body and the mucous membranes connected with it and also the closed cavities of the body. An *epithiloma:* a carcinoma of the palate."

Clemens sits.

CLEMENS Cancer. Why wasn't I shown this?

FRED Badeau didn't want you to know the severity.

CLEMENS Why would he protect me of all people?

FRED He has his reasons. Listen to me. You love my father. I can tell that.

CLEMENS I admire—no, I love this man. To be in his presence is—

FRED How can Father write a book? Let him have his last days in peace. Let him die. He has perhaps two weeks left. Let those days be spent in peace.

CLEMENS But the book—I've spent a fortune of my own money.

FRED If there is to be a book, then let us—you and I— extract it from him in the time he has left. At least we'll be kind.

CLEMENS Badeau has shown me the work he claims your father has done. It's hopeless . . .

Fred gives Clemens pages.

FRED These are pages I've taken from Father while Badeau has been out.

CLEMENS (*Reads*) "Slavery was an institution that required unusual guarantees for its security wherever it existed; hence the people of the South were dependent upon keeping control of the general government to secure the perpetuation of their favorite institution."

FRED That was the voice of my father ten days ago.

CLEMENS But Badeau said *this* was the voice of your father—

FRED These terrible flowery pages are forgeries by Badeau. This is the truth of the man. Badeau knows this. He is waiting for my father to die—

CLEMENS No—he's your father's trusted aide—

FRED He knows my father's death is inevitable. He means to take over the book—take it away from you, if necessary—publish his own book. Have his book be the only book.

CLEMENS I can't believe you.

FRED I beg you to fire Badeau and allow me to take over—

Badeau bangs on the door.

BADEAU (*Off*) What are you saying in there? You can't bar me from here—that room is my workplace! What are you doing in there?

Clemens opens the door. Gerhardt looks in.

GERHARDT Time?

Clemens closes the door. He shows Badeau the doctor's report.

CLEMENS Is this true?

BADEAU Yes. The cancer does exist. (*To Fred, snidely*) The publisher must have left.

48

CLEMENS   Don't you have any sense of alarm?

BADEAU   With the general's strength—his unfortunately long-lived family—this cancer can linger for years. We're all dying in one way or another. That doesn't mean that we become paralyzed. You know you'll die but that doesn't stop you from writing your new book. How is it coming? Published next month. Are the reports good? I hear nothing but wonderful—

CLEMENS   The doctors who wrote this report—

BADEAU   Doctors want to get their hooks in you. I know this man.

BUCK, *a young man whose eyes are red from lack of sleep, from despair, appears.*

BUCK   Father—

FRED   Don't come in here.

BADEAU   Get out.

GERHARDT   Is it time?

The door shuts.

USG   Buck? Buck?

USG rails.

BUCK   Yessir, it's Buck! Could I just get you to sign one—

BADEAU   You're upsetting him.

USG   Get out.

BUCK   It needs his signature.

CLEMENS   Let me see that—

BUCK No!

USG No no—

BADEAU You're not to come here.

BUCK To sign this one paper! It's a foolproof scheme to earn back the money.

FRED You're the reason we're in the trouble we're in. You're the proof of a fool.

CLEMENS You have all of New York to argue in—go out into the park.

USG Emperor! Defend me! Where are you?

BUCK I'm trying to restore—

FRED I didn't squander a million dollars.

BUCK I'm trying to make good on a new investment. But I need his signature.

CLEMENS Your father has signed enough paper from you—

BUCK It's a good investment—

CLEMENS I am taking care of his investments.

BADEAU You are?

CLEMENS I've just decided.

BUCK You can't move in on—

CLEMENS You squandered one million dollars.

Mrs. G runs in.

MRS. G Is Buck here? How are you? There was no fire in the kitchen and no food either. Oh darling—are you eating? Look at you.

FRED He has no right to be here!

MRS. G Don't say a word against Buck. He didn't know.

FRED Always Buck—Buck's always right—I'm just Little Dog. Thanks to Buck, Father's sunk so low he has to sell his life to make any money. Buck's staying with his rich in-laws. I have to live here in this mausoleum of memory because I have no money to live anywhere else—let us recollect, let us recollect till you want to go mad.

BUCK Mother, I just need Father to sign this one paper.

MRS. G Dear, Buck wants you to do one little—

USG rails.

CLEMENS He's signed enough trouble from you. Get out.

MRS. G Don't say anything against Buck.

FRED Buck's always been the favorite.

BUCK Father. Mother. I am heartily sorry and am trying to repair any financial unpleasantness, and this man—

FRED Financial unpleasantness you call it? Get out of here.

MRS. G Don't say a word against Buck.

Nell opens the door.

NELL Mother? It's Reverend Newman all the way up from Washington.

Gerhardt peers in.

GERHARDT Mr. Clemens!

CLEMENS Not now!

The door shuts.

MRS. G Reverend Newman wants to see you!

BUCK Nell! Talk some sense to them—

NELL Don't talk to me—you lost my husband's money—

USG rails.

BADEAU He doesn't want to see the reverend.

MRS. G He's come to give spiritual comfort.

BADEAU We're trying to work. (*To Clemens*) The missus wants the general baptized.

MRS. G If you don't have time for a psalm, I pity all of you.

NELL He's come all the way up from Washington.

MRS. G Lyss, you've never been baptized. Please do this for me. It's just a little bit of water to you, but it means the difference for all eternity.

USG No!

BADEAU Go!

Mrs. G and Nell go.

FRED Buck willfully pissed away one million dollars.

Gerhardt looks in.

GERHARDT Is it—?

CLEMENS No!

The door shuts.

BUCK We were all hoodwinked by Mr. Ward. I had bad advice then. I have good advice now. Please sign this paper.

CLEMENS He's too sick.

BUCK Then stop writing this book and get him to a hospital.

BADEAU It's too late! If I was around last year, I would've insisted that the carcinoma of his palate be tended to. It could've been removed at any hospital, but someone prevented it. Who was it?

FRED Buck!

BADEAU Buck!

BUCK I didn't know how ill he was.

CLEMENS You!

Mrs. G opens the door.

MRS. G Don't say a word against Buck—

Gerhardt looks in. Mrs. G and Nell come in. Nell closes the door.

MRS. G The reverend left you a Bible! Isn't that sweet! It's his own Bible that he used in the war!

BADEAU Someone canceled the operation. Buck. Buck wouldn't allow the operation because he needed his father's fame to give his tawdry scheme credibility!

FRED You listened to Buck. Don't listen to Little Dog.

NELL If I had been in America—

BUCK I didn't believe he was sick—

USG rails.

BADEAU It's all right, sir.

MRS. G Don't say anything against Buck.

BADEAU   Your son Buck prevented the operation.

FRED   Stick up for Buck! Don't listen to me.

BADEAU   Because Buck needed the general to go to Vanderbilt and beg for money to float a sinking firm.

NELL   You ruined my husband.

MRS. G   Buck was trying his best.

BADEAU   And Buck lost all your money and the money of everyone else who was unfortunate enough to fly into his web.

BUCK   I had bad advice but now I have confidence in myself.

CLEMENS   Confidence!

BADEAU   A confidence game!

MRS. G   He had bad advice, that's all.

BADEAU   Buck willfully pissed away one million of your dollars.

BUCK   I'll get it back. I'll restore—just sign.

MRS. G   He'll get it back.

BADEAU   How? Buck prevented the operation—

BUCK   If you don't need me—

BADEAU   We don't.

CLEMENS   I just stopped by on my way to Philadelphia.

MRS. G   Come back later, dear Buck. Come back then.

FRED   You're not needed here.

BUCK If I'm so superfluous then I'll go down to the Academy of Music to get a ticket for Adelina Patti's farewell concert—Nell, would you like to come?

NELL Go to a concert hall and have people pointing me out? "Her father stole money from the son of Commodore Vanderbilt."

MRS. G But your father is innocent.

NELL It's not what the world thinks. I can't go—

BUCK Just a single. Oh—I find myself short.

CLEMENS Be careful where you walk—no! We don't have any spare money. Get out. We are working here—

BUCK I need money for a ticket.

CLEMENS There is no money for tickets to Adelina Patti.

BUCK But this is Adelina Patti's farewell tour!

CLEMENS —her latest farewell tour—

BUCK No. After Adelina Patti sings tonight, no one will ever hear that sublime voice again. That voice will only live in memory! I have to be there to remember her!

CLEMENS The vanity!

BUCK It's pennies I need—

CLEMENS (*Flinging coins*) Then take pennies!

Buck gets down on all fours to pick up the coins.

BUCK I would like to sit in a box. That's dollars.

CLEMENS Be grateful for the pennies.

BUCK Do you know who I am?

CLEMENS Unfortunately I do. We are trying to finish a book that will drown you in all the dollars you will ever need—

BUCK (*Standing*) You talk about money. We never see any money. Mother, do you have any money? We had a million dollars.

Buck goes. Gerhardt peers in.

GERHARDT Is it—

The door closes.

CLEMENS These pages you showed me—did you write this and this?

BADEAU Yes. I did write this and this and this. What am I supposed to do? He's inaccessible. He sits here in a stupor. You keep saying fortune fortune. The book is being written for the poor fools who served under him. They will take what we give them. You delegated authority to me. I did what I thought you would do.

CLEMENS That is the worst insult—

BADEAU Yes, I am writing him. And why not!

CLEMENS But I don't want your voice—

BADEAU I'm protecting him. I sent copies of the early pages to England to my great friend Matthew Arnold, who said, "The best things said and done in the world are missing from the pages—"

NELL I know him. He's been to my house. What about Henry James? He's an American of a proper sort. Mr. James could help Father elevate his style.

MRS. G All the literary lights flock to her house.

BADEAU Arnold said, "Where is the poetry of war?" I was consul in London. I am in touch with these men. "Where is the glory—the grandeur?" This is too flat and too prosaic. Plus, the language is gone astray in the continued misuse of *shall* and *will* and *should* and *would*. Pity the poor general—the favorite of Mars, defeated by the literary gods. You hired me to assist this man who is completely nonliterary engage in the sacred task of writing a book. Do business with me. I will save you. I was this man's aide. I am his official biographer. I am offering you an out.

CLEMENS Surrender? Never. He'd never surrender.

BADEAU But he'd know when to backtrack and take another path to achieve *victory*. You are stealing money from me. He wanted me to write his book. It takes a great writer to write the life he has lead. It takes a writer—

CLEMENS Of your skills and credentials?

BADEAU I was about to say *not* of *your* skills and credentials.

CLEMENS But I want it in his words—not your words—

MRS. G He's kept the general drugged even when he isn't in pain. He's kept him only on morphine while we've been writing. He's locked Lyss in this chamber for hours at a time—

BADEAU The man is in pain—

CLEMENS Mr. Badeau, I think I've given you enough rope. I see what you're up to. You have been sabotaging this project from the start. You want your own memoirs of the general to be the only book published.

BADEAU I resent your insinuations.

CLEMENS They don't sound like insinuations to me. If I am insinuating anything, it's that you can't get out of here quick enough for me.

BADEAU You're jettisoning the book?

CLEMENS I am taking it over! I will produce the book! I will find a way to the general's memory.

MRS. G (*To Badeau*) You hear him. Go go go go—

BADEAU Are you firing me?

CLEMENS When my tour is over, I am giving this all my time. You have not done that which I have hired you for. Go.

MRS. G Go.

BADEAU I'll destroy your book with slander. I have friends in high places. I'll say the general is dead—

CLEMENS And I'll wheel him to the window and parade him up and down Fifth Avenue.

BADEAU I'll say the book's a forgery perpetrated by you. People will believe it—

CLEMENS And I'll show them your pages. People can tell a forgery.

BADEAU You're a buffoon. I heard about your readings from your latest gooseberry travesty—colored people rafting down rivers—nakedness—things about dead chickens.

CLEMENS That's true but you've got the wrong berry.

BADEAU I don't think Gutenberg invented the printing press to spew out pages about dead chickens—and white children floating naked down rivers on rafts with Negroes.

CLEMENS   We really don't know what hopes Gutenberg had for his—

BADEAU   And darkies speaking in minstrel dialect. Is that what you want your husband's book to be?

CLEMENS   It's not minstrel. There are at least four different dialects I've used in the book. I'm very proud of—I'm trying to portray accurately—

BADEAU   Accurately?

CLEMENS   So you didn't like my book?

BADEAU   My friends whom I trust call it trash.

CLEMENS   If it's trash, it's my trash and it's the best trash.

BADEAU   It's all part of your revenge.

CLEMENS   Revenge?

BADEAU   Refresh my memory? What side did you fight on?

CLEMENS   For two noble weeks I fought for the South. Nothing surpassed my experience in the army as my leaving it.

BADEAU   Then you deserted!

CLEMENS   My finest hour.

BADEAU   (*To Mrs. G*)   A rebel. A deserter. No wonder your husband resists you—you've let the enemy into our house disguised as the Trojan horse of money. He wants to slander the general's memory forever. Make a fool of him. It's been his plan all along to take over the book.

MRS. G   You're taking over the book?

BADEAU To make the general a laughingstock. Oh, I can just hear the general spouting talk like Mr. Bones.

NELL You're not making Father speak in a minstrel dialect?

BADEAU You'll see. He'll make your father a figure of derision.

CLEMENS The minute I start writing this book you can put me in the street. It'll be in his voice or not at all. Don't worry. I couldn't capture the purity of his voice. The reviewers are right. I write about eccentric people, grotesque people—in other words, Americans. I could never write his book. He has a sanity and a purpose. He is a great man. It'll be in his words or not at all. Get out!

BADEAU He'll never live long enough to finish it.

CLEMENS I'll take care of him.

BADEAU Really? With your famous bad luck?

CLEMENS I didn't realize my luck was famous.

BADEAU As with everything you love, the general will die on your watch.

MRS. G Don't say that.

BADEAU This man can't protect anything—his son—

CLEMENS What are you saying?

BADEAU Your own son—

CLEMENS I want you to leave—

MRS. G What about your son?

BADEAU His own son died on his watch.

CLEMENS Go!

BADEAU He kept his son out in the cold. The boy contracted pneumonia and died. He'll kill the general. The general survived the war. He won't survive this angel of death.

USG Is he the one who wants to kill me?

CLEMENS Get out.

BADEAU Didn't you also have something to do with your brother's death? A steamer exploding on the river—you haven't written about any of this. Amnesia like the general's? *Paramnesia* it's called in *Diseases of Memory*. You both forget the nightmares—why haven't you written about it?

CLEMENS Get out or I'll kill you—I mean that—

MRS. G Who gave you such horrid information?

BADEAU I ask around. I get my information. I store it up. One thing I've learned from the general. Know your enemy. I knew it'd come to this. You fire me and I am your sworn enemy. One day the general will be dead and you'll come to me. You'll need me. I have papers no one else has seen. I have information no one else knows. I know information about him that even he doesn't know; I won't help you because I'll have my own book.

CLEMENS Ma'am, would you sign here?

MRS. G What is this? I don't have my glasses.

CLEMENS I'm transfering ownership of the general's book to you—no one can sue him for any profits—oh God, I actually believe this book will be written?

FRED Do it, Mother.

MRS. G   I own Lyss's memories? I like that.

She kisses USG on the head and signs the paper. Clemens signs it as witness.

CLEMENS   Fred, would you witness?

Fred signs.

CLEMENS (*To Badeau*)   Would you care to sign as a witness?

BADEAU   Wait till my tongue unleashes itself to its gigantic length. My tongue is forked and poisoned and fast and deadly and quick. (*To Mrs. G*) Will you not stick up for me?

MRS. G   Why?

BADEAU   Because I have put up with your stupidity all these years—

MRS. G   Go. Go go go go go.

BADEAU   You'll be sorry you excluded me from this project.

MRS. G   I want you to go, I want you to go!

FRED   Are we doing the right thing?

NELL   Mother, don't be rash.

BADEAU   Do you want me to stay? One last chance.

CLEMENS   No.

BADEAU   Choose.

USG   Go!

MRS. G   I want you to go.

USG   Go.

BADEAU General. I put a curse on your memory.

Badeau gathers all his books and records and pages in his arms.

CLEMENS Nothing of his, nothing of his—

BADEAU I need nothing here.

Badeau goes, limping.

CLEMENS I always thought Rumpelstiltskin a fiction—Gerhardt? Where are you? Has anyone seen the man who was out here? Gerhardt? Gerhardt?

Gerhardt is not there. Clemens closes the door.

MRS. G Did your son die? Were you responsible?

CLEMENS It's something I live with every day. We all live with something.

NELL You haven't written about it . . .

CLEMENS Just because it happened doesn't mean it's accessible. My little son—Langdon—oh, this is back in the seventies—over ten years ago—I was taking my son for a ride around Hartford in my carriage—he was two—a winter's day—I was working on a book—I got engrossed in my work—I didn't notice we had been out driving for hours—by the time we got back my son had a chill that turned into pneumonia. He was dead a while later—my work always ahead of my family—my life—my work killed my son. You're not going to die on my watch. I am going to atone for that death by your life—

Pause.

MRS. G Mr. Clemens, I trust you.

FRED I trust you.

63

NELL I guess I trust you.

CLEMENS Sir, my entire future is resting on your memory. Let us retrospect.

MRS. G Where's my pencil?

NELL & FRED Let us retrospect. Father! Retrospect!

CLEMENS Let us retrospect!

USG It's a closed door—Where is the emperor?

Gerhardt opens the door and enters.

GERHARDT It must be time?

CLEMENS Yes! Yes! Why not. I have a surprise.

Gerhardt comes in, carrying a large clay model of the head of USG.

GERHARDT Sir, I came today to show you the portrait bust— sir?

CLEMENS Remember Mr. Gerhardt?

GERHARDT It's my masterpiece.

CLEMENS After Gerhardt sets it in bronze, he will photograph it and print it on the frontispiece of your—do you hear me?

GERHARDT I have decided I will add the general's body to this head—perhaps nude like Michelangelo's *David*.

MRS. G Never!

GERHARDT Then perhaps clad in a toga like a Roman hero but not small—big—taller than this Statue of Freedom lady they're erecting in New York harbor. Why would we take France's hand-me-downs? Erect a statue of the man who brought America together—who fought to make us one.

64

MRS. G Yes—wonderful, except that's not his nose. You're not putting that nose in New York harbor or on the front of a book—Fred! Nell! Look at Father—

FRED That's not my father!

NELL That nose!

GERHARDT The nose is perfect!

MRS. G Let me fix the nose.

GERHARDT Don't you dare touch it!

MRS. G I know his nose better than you.

They grapple over the clay model, pulling it apart. Gerhardt is left holding the nose.

GERHARDT No!

MRS. G (*Weeps*) Watch out! He's knocked over West Point, which is now mixed up with Mexico.

USG Japan.

CLEMENS It's under control. Gerhardt—go—wait for me outside. It's only clay—

GERHARDT Only clay? It was my masterpiece—the nose is perfect—

USG Japan.

Gerhardt exits, weeping, sculpting the clay. USG cries out.

MRS. G Let me give you a shot. A cold—change of seasons—spring is coming. We all have allergies.

Mrs. G injects USG with a shot of brandy. Golden light. The Emperor and Empress of Japan reappear.

THE EMPEROR OF JAPAN I am the emperor of Japan
   I am the throne of chrysanthemum
   I am shadow
   I am light
   I am memory I am memory I am memory I am memory

USG You've come back!

THE EMPEROR OF JAPAN I've decided to forgive you.

THE EMPRESS OF JAPAN I apologize for my husband. He does
   not know how to behave. You mustn't ruin your friendship
   over a fan. There are so many fans, and we have an idea—
   the play that was presented at the banquet in your honor
   that was the story of your life—if you read that you would
   know who you were.

USG Get it for me!

CLEMENS Remember—that's all. Just tell what happened in
   your words—that's all I want—does he hear me?

USG gasps.

THE EMPEROR OF JAPAN You've read my play. Tell him the
   story of my play. Give him something. Speak to him.

MRS. G Take the Bible that the Reverend Newman brought.
   Read the psalms. Find the solace—

USG takes the Bible.

USG Is this the story of my life?

THE EMPEROR OF JAPAN As presented in Japan!

CLEMENS I'll be back in three weeks. My reading tour over—
   I'll be here—we'll get the book out of him. Sir, together
   we can do it.

Clemens starts to go.

USG (*With difficulty*) I think . . .

CLEMENS Yes?

USG I can help you.

Everyone freezes, astonished.

CLEMENS You spoke.

THE EMPEROR OF JAPAN Don't be nervous. You have a contract.

USG We have a contract.

CLEMENS Yes!

USG Let's get to work.

FRED Father is so honorable—

CLEMENS Sir, I must tell you I am very moved—I have patience—I knew you'd come through—Mrs. Grant, pencil, paper—

USG Let us recollect.

THE EMPEROR OF JAPAN I'll hold my play open so you can read it—begin.

The Emperor of Japan holds up the script like cue cards. Japanese hieroglyphs.

USG I was born in a cave—

CLEMENS Better than a log cabin—

USG On the edge of the universe—

CLEMENS Where would that be?

USG   And after I had two sons I retired to my cave to meditate and thank great Buddha for what he had given me.

CLEMENS   I've met two of your sons, but I thought you had three sons.

USG   My two sons, Nathan North and Samuel South.

CLEMENS   What—

USG   They hated each other. Each wanted to rule the land on the edge of eternity. They each assembled great hordes of men and fought each other with such brutality that they ripped the land in two—two masses of land as high as the Fujimin Mountains and as deep as the China Sea ripped in two.

THE EMPEROR OF JAPAN   Do it with gestures!

The Emperor and Empress of Japan play music. The Empress of Japan dances to illustrate the text.

USG   The land was covered with so much blood the rest of the world began to tilt and then drown. Do something, do something, I heard the world cry. I stepped out of my cave and, with my sword, to stop the bloodshed, killed both my sons. I put one foot on the mountain Fujiyama, the other foot on the mountain Asama-yama, and dragged the two sundered masses of land together. The people fell down and worshiped me. My country was made one. It is the end of all war. I was taken into heaven and welcomed by my noble predecessors, whom I join in eternity in the highest part of heaven.

Silence. The Emperor of Japan pats USG on the back.

THE EMPEROR OF JAPAN   Very good.

Pause.

CLEMENS I imagined a different story.

MRS. G Is it too late to bring back Badeau?

CLEMENS Sir, this is no one's life.

USG My friend said it was.

THE EMPEROR OF JAPAN My priests told me your life— granted, there are some changes I made for the Japanese taste and the fact that no one in Japan knows who you are except me.

MRS. G That's the story of his life in Japan. A "Noh play" it's called, and no play is exactly what it was.

CLEMENS Sir, I can't countenance this. We're going to have to forgo the book and get you to a hospital. I'm very sorry it hasn't worked out.

USG I'm not going to a hospital! What did you tell me?

USG flings the Bible on the floor in a rage.

THE EMPEROR OF JAPAN I had no knowledge. My priests would not let me hear any more pages about America. They say America is a dangerous idea. I did invent a few details, but I'm allowed. Are all Americans so literal?

USG You, you, you, what's your name?

CLEMENS Clemens.

USG I have to tell you. I have no memory of anything and that book didn't ring a bell. It's something someone I thought was a friend gave me.

THE EMPEROR OF JAPAN I am a friend!

USG Friends don't treat friends that way.

CLEMENS We want the best for you.

MRS. G Oh my Victor—

FRED Let Father die. Let the cancer run its course—

MRS. G He does not have that word!

CLEMENS I have a reading in Philadelphia tonight—

Harrison returns holding the drugs in glass bottles.

HARRISON The cocaine, the morphine, the cannabis.

FRED Give that to me!

MRS. G Let me hold it—

NELL I have a blinding headache—

They all take a whiff of the drugs. Clemens is in despair. Badeau appears.

BADEAU Have you changed your mind?

Clemens and USG look at each other.

CLEMENS Have I? Is it possible?

USG Stay with me. We are the two most powerful men in the world.

USG extends his hand. Clemens and the Emperor of Japan go to USG. They both clasp USG's hand.

CLEMENS Why, thank you, sir. We're going to be fine.

Clemens walks to Badeau and confronts him. Badeau goes. USG, still holding the Emperor of Japan's hand, looks at the Emperor. USG is frightened. Clemens is happy.

The Empress of Japan bangs a gong.

CURTAIN

ACT TWO

Darkness. Then golden light. The room is filled with flowers. USG stands. The Emperor of Japan sits in USG's chair, the Empress of Japan by his side.

USG   Was being with you the last time I was ever happy?

THE EMPEROR OF JAPAN   I hope so.

USG   Being in a new strange place but liking it.

THE EMPRESS OF JAPAN   Why?

USG   Country beautifully cultivated. Scenery grand. The people from the highest to the lowest, the most kindly . . . the most cleanly in the world. Meeting you. You wanted nothing from me. We were the two most powerful men in the world. It made me smile.

THE EMPEROR OF JAPAN   I wanted you to be happy in Japan.

USG   Oh, I was.

THE EMPRESS OF JAPAN   We are very happy visiting you.

USG   Could you stay?

THE EMPRESS OF JAPAN   We would love to! Could we?

THE EMPEROR OF JAPAN   I cannot leave my country.

USG   I understand. I apologize.

THE EMPEROR OF JAPAN   For what?

USG   My memory. You asked for things I couldn't give you.

THE EMPEROR OF JAPAN   I apologize.

USG   For what?

THE EMPEROR OF JAPAN   For my solution. Giving you my play.

USG   But you wanted to help.

THE EMPEROR OF JAPAN   I did.

THE EMPRESS OF JAPAN   He did. You did it very well.

USG   It felt good.

THE EMPEROR OF JAPAN   You told it most admirably.

USG   Could I have a photograph of you?

THE EMPEROR OF JAPAN   No representations of me are allowed.

USG   That's a shame. I'd like a picture of the two of us, our arms slung over each other's shoulders, looking into the camera. We could each hold a glass of whiskey and a cigar. We could have a map of the world between us. One half yours. One half mine.

THE EMPEROR OF JAPAN   I would like to be the face of your savior. When you need help, think of me.

Bells toll in the street.

USG   What's going on out there?

The Emperor and Empress of Japan go to the window.

THE EMPEROR OF JAPAN   People are crowding outside this house—

THE EMPRESS OF JAPAN   Up onto Fifth Avenue—

THE EMPEROR OF JAPAN   Back into Central Park—

USG   What's happened? Why are they there?

THE EMPEROR OF JAPAN   Funeral bells.

USG   Whose funeral?

THE EMPEROR OF JAPAN   There are hundreds—

THE EMPRESS OF JAPAN   Maybe thousands—

THE EMPEROR OF JAPAN   —of people out in the street.

USG   Who else lives on this block?

THE EMPEROR OF JAPAN   It's you. Yes, it's your funeral.

USG   Have I died?

THE EMPEROR OF JAPAN   Not yet. They've come to be with you. I remember when my father was dying. Thousands of people stood in front of the palace.

THE EMPRESS OF JAPAN   A deathwatch. That's what they call it.

THE EMPEROR OF JAPAN   This is your deathwatch.

USG   Is it a bloodthirsty deathwatch?

THE EMPEROR OF JAPAN   They're very quiet. Very Japanese. Some of them have on their old uniforms. They carry flags. They have signs.

USG   Saying that I'm a thief? That I stole money from Mr. Vanderbilt? What do the signs say?

THE EMPEROR OF JAPAN   I'm so sorry. I can't read. My readers read to me.

THE EMPRESS OF JAPAN   The signs say they love you. They're with you.

USG   Nothing like imminent death to revive affection.

USG sits in his chair.

THE EMPEROR OF JAPAN   You can read?

THE EMPRESS OF JAPAN   I can't sit around that drafty palace all day listening to old men read to me. Of course I can.

THE EMPEROR OF JAPAN   You never told me you could read.

THE EMPRESS OF JAPAN   I read all the papers. Badeau—that horrible man—gave the doctor's reports to the newspapers. He's trying to destroy your book.

The Emperor of Japan hands her a newspaper.

THE EMPEROR OF JAPAN   I don't believe you.

The Empress of Japan takes the paper.

THE EMPRESS OF JAPAN   "The general will tragically die before completing his awaited memoirs."

THE EMPEROR OF JAPAN   You can read.

USG   She can read.

THE EMPEROR OF JAPAN   I am shocked.

Mournful tolling. Then sounds of commotion. The light changes. Clemens enters carrying newspapers. Mrs. G follows.

MRS. G   What's that commotion out in the street?

CLEMENS   Badeau has done his business. See the evening papers. The general is dying. Badeau's revealed the doctor's report.

MRS. G   It's not true.

USG   But it is.

Fred runs in.

74

FRED What's going on?

CLEMENS Badeau's poison. See the paper—

FRED (*Reads*) "Will tragically die before finishing his awaited memoirs"—

CLEMENS How can we sell books when the papers say there will be no book?

FRED People know the truth. The truth's been spoken. Is there any food in the house?

CLEMENS And does speaking the truth make you feel any better? Or solve any problems? That's the worst thing about the truth. Just because you say it, doesn't mean you're going to feel better. Sir, Badeau is trying to trump you—he wants you to die so only his book will be published. He's the enemy. You can't allow him to do this to you. We have to trump him. We have to wage a full frontal attack on Badeau and prove him a liar. One page. Two pages. Anything from you is valuable. I am back. My tour is over. I am yours. Sir, do you hear me?

THE EMPEROR OF JAPAN Of course you hear him.

USG I'm staying very quiet.

CLEMENS Has he had any lucidity in the past three weeks?

MRS. G Some. He wrote these pages.

Mrs. G hands Clemens a few pages. Clemens reads.

CLEMENS "Mr. Lincoln gained influence over men by making them feel it was a pleasure to serve him. He preferred yielding his own wishes to gratify others, rather than to insist upon having his own way. It distressed him to disappoint others. In matters of public duty, however, he had what he wished, but in the least offensive way . . . Mr. Stanton, the secretary of war, cared nothing for the feelings of others. In fact it seemed to be pleasanter to him to disappoint than to gratify." But this is him at his best.

Fred picks up a dish.

MRS. G   Don't eat that marrow pudding. That's for him!

FRED   Are you aware there's not a crumb of bread in the kitchen?

Fred goes.

MRS. G   Harrison was supposed to shop—Harrison!

Harrison brings in more flowers.

MRS. G   Put those in the front parlor.

HARRISON   I want to put them where he can see them.

MRS. G   The flowers make him sick—that odor already rancid—

Nell comes in.

NELL   I can't get out the front door. The crowds are too big.

CLEMENS   Then go out the back door.

NELL   Only servants use the back door. I'm going to the steamship company to see if Algy's arrived with the children to surprise me. Yes! Surprise!

MRS. G   (*To Clemens*)   Mr. Clemens, you have daughters. Could you give my daughter some advice?

CLEMENS   Don't marry an Englishman.

Nell goes.

CLEMENS   Sir, we're waging a full frontal attack on Badeau. I'm going to shake this book out of you. We're going to beat time. Remember General Wallace's book? *Ben-Hur*?

USG   No *Ben-Hur*!

CLEMENS   You're in a chariot race with time. You're going to win.

USG   I don't know your name.

CLEMENS   Clemens. Are we back to this?

THE EMPEROR OF JAPAN   Mutsu-hito. But it is not my real name.

CLEMENS   Let us recollect. Tell us the story of Ulysses S. Grant.

USG   That's not my real name either.

CLEMENS   What's he saying?

MRS. G   There's no reason to go into that.

CLEMENS   Sir, what did you mean—not your real name?

USG   My real name is Hiram.

MRS. G   Hiram Ulysses. No need to go into this—

THE EMPEROR OF JAPAN   Tell me.

CLEMENS   Tell me.

USG   When I was going away to West Point I saw my baggage with the initials *H.U.G.* stenciled on—I said, I can't lead men with the initials *H.U.G.* I dropped the Hiram right then—changed it all to Ulysses.

THE EMPEROR OF JAPAN & CLEMENS   The *S*?

USG Pulled the *S* out of nowhere. But it worked. At West Point they called me Uncle Sam. Do you have a real name?

CLEMENS I've told you—

THE EMPEROR OF JAPAN God.

USG Has a ring to it.

CLEMENS The armistice—we have to get to the end of the war. I've promised two volumes. With editing and work we have one volume. We have to have enough to fill out a second volume. I'll pad it with maps, lots of maps.

Fred comes in, eating a slice of cake.

FRED Father!

CLEMENS This room is off-limits to high jinks!

FRED I just opened the front door to go out and there stands an old lady with the brightest china-blue eyes holding a Viennese chocolate cake she made for Father! It is sublime—

Mrs. G runs after him.

MRS. G It might be poisoned—you don't know—he still has enemies—people still want him to die! The assassination— we were the targets that night—not Lincoln—people still want us dead.

Mrs. G tries to grab the cake. Fred turns away, eating.

CLEMENS You were the targets that night?

THE EMPEROR OF JAPAN You were the targets that night?

MRS. G Yes, we were supposed to go to the theater that night but the children got sick and we left Washington and came up to our villa in New Jersey. Stop eating that cake.

78

FRED We saved Father's life.

MRS. G Don't talk with your mouth full.

Mrs. G grabs the cake. Fred trips over the stacks of paper.

CLEMENS You've knocked over Chattanooga—Vicksburg—oh God—

FRED Father, if we have to die, taste this.

CLEMENS You've got chocolate all over Gettysburg. He can't have any cake.

FRED There's no food in the house. Let me live off cakes left at our door. If they're going to be so generous, perhaps I could put a menu on the door saying what I'd like.

CLEMENS You're the incarnation of chaos. I try to bring order here and you—

They straighten up.

FRED One more bite. No poison at all. Look—

Fred gags, chokes, falls to the floor in agony.

FRED I'm dying—Egypt, I am dying—poisoned! Aaaagh—

THE EMPEROR OF JAPAN Help him!

MRS. G Fred!

The Empress of Japan screams. Mrs. G leaps forward.

MRS. G Mr. Clemens, do something!

Fred stands up, laughing.

CLEMENS Oh God.

MRS. G Don't do that.

FRED Father! I'm trying to make you laugh.

CLEMENS Get out of here. We are trying to do the armistice—

He pushes Fred out of the room.

CLEMENS (*To USG*) Let's get to work. Is it the prospect of the blank page that's put you in this state? Sometimes when I'm about to write, all that whiteness gives me the shivers. Don't be afraid—one page—every day one page—bit by bit, tell your life—don't be afraid. Four months ago you said you could do it.

Harrison brings in more flowers.

MRS. G Put them in the parlor.

HARRISON No room.

MRS. G Put them in the dining room.

HARRISON No room.

MRS. G Get rid of them.

CLEMENS They're expressions of love.

MRS. G Throw them out in the street.

CLEMENS You can't do that. Revolutions have started over less—

MRS. G I look at these flowers and see only the money people spent. If they love us, why don't they send us the money? Are there any flowers from Mr. Vanderbilt? Maybe he's forgiven us.

Harrison goes, followed by Mrs. G. Clemens takes out a book.

CLEMENS *Diseases of Memory.* Was Badeau right? According to this book memory reacts to stimulus. The way to his memory consists in finding the correct stimulus. It's very scientific—

Gerhardt sneaks in the door and starts laying strips of gauze over USG's face.

THE EMPEROR OF JAPAN (*Curious*)   What is this?

USG   What is this!

Clemens looks up.

CLEMENS   What in God's name—

GERHARDT   I happily do his bust. I am grateful for the honor. When he dies—I would like to do the death mask.

CLEMENS   Let's get to that when it comes.

GERHARDT   You can smell the death on him. I want the exclusive rights now.

CLEMENS   You are being premature. The rights to the death mask will be negotiated at the proper time.

GERHARDT   If we make an agreement now, it would give everything clarity when the worst happens. It would make me feel secure if I knew I was doing the death mask. It will sell—all those people out there—all over America people will buy a death mask. If you don't give me the rights I will stop the bust.

CLEMENS   I will give you the rights when he dies. Not a moment before. Go! Go!

GERHARDT   I have to make a nickel. You can't be the only one making money.

CLEMENS   Me make money? I have a talent for not making money. I'm Midas in reverse.

81

Gerhardt leaves.

CLEMENS Let us recollect—Sir—let's start anywhere—the truce. Is there any truth to the legend about signing the truce with Lee under the apple tree? Did he surrender his sword and then you gave it back to him?

THE EMPEROR OF JAPAN Answer him.

USG War produces many fictions—no no—can't.

CLEMENS Maybe—the proper stimulus. Harrison! Harrison!

HARRISON Yes?

CLEMENS Harrison, do you know anyone in New York who served with the general—someone I could get in here?

HARRISON General Sherman was here.

CLEMENS I know that didn't work.

HARRISON General Wallace—

USG *Ben-Hur*!

CLEMENS No *Ben-Hur*—don't worry—

HARRISON I don't know what other friends could trigger his memory.

CLEMENS Were you in the war?

HARRISON Yes sir. Served under him, sir.

USG Where?

HARRISON Cold Harbor.

USG Cold Harbor?

CLEMENS Cold Harbor?

THE EMPEROR OF JAPAN   Cold Harbor?

USG   Are you a ghost?

Mrs. G runs in.

HARRISON   I don't think so—unless maybe I did die at Cold Harbor along with everybody else. Maybe I am a ghost. That would explain the last twenty years.

CLEMENS   You served at Cold Harbor?

USG is violently disturbed.

MRS. G   There'll be nothing of Cold Harbor in this book. This is a happy book designed to sell millions of copies.

USG   No Cold Harbor.

THE EMPEROR OF JAPAN   What is Cold Harbor? What is Cold Harbor?

USG   I can't tell you.

MRS. G   No talk about Cold Harbor!

Nell and Fred come in.

NELL   Mother, we're saved!

Gerhardt peers in.

GERHARDT   The treatment only takes half an hour—

The door closes.

NELL   Thank God I went to the steamship office! I ran into Mrs. Pierrepont! She's chairlady for the pedestal people and she's here!

MRS. G   In this house!

CLEMENS   The who? Can't you see we're working?

NELL   She's raising money for the pedestal on which to set the Statue of Liberty. The United States government won't give one cent for—

CLEMENS   That two-hundred-foot woman France is dumping on America?

NELL   She needs a pedestal.

CLEMENS   Mrs. Pierrepont?

NELL   The Statue of Liberty.

CLEMENS   Why not? Everyone else in New York puts themselves on a pedestal.

NELL   Mrs. Pierrepont was so sad to hear about Father's condition that she actually wants Father's name on the subscription list! It's the beginning of our redemption! Sign here! Harrison, will you make Mrs. Pierrepont and the pedestal people feel we have some capabilities as hosts—

CLEMENS   We are working here—

NELL   This won't take but a moment. Sign here!

CLEMENS   Let me see this letter. Your father's got in enough trouble signing pieces of paper pushed under his nose.

FRED   What kind of city would want a two-hundred-foot concierge standing in its harbor?

NELL   Can you imagine what that monstrosity will look like? Another reason for my husband to laugh at America—

As USG signs his name:

CLEMENS (*To us*)   We need a statue of Adam at the entrance of America. A naked wild man holding a club. General,

84

weren't you and I once both primitive men? Look at us now. You living in a mansion off Fifth Avenue. I'm in an overdecorated palace in Hartford. What happened to us? Oh, to arrive as an immigrant here. Forget your past. A whole new self. To be Sam Clemens again—on the Mississippi—waiting for life to start.

NELL   Put a little note—"P.S. looking forward to meeting you."

CLEMENS   He signs his name. That's enough—

Nell takes the letter.

NELL   You should be very proud, Father, that we're not barred from every social list. Maybe if we do enough good works, we'll be accepted back into the social graces of New York.

CLEMENS   Don't keep the pedestal people waiting, Mrs. Sartoris.

NELL   Mother, please come and pay homage to Mrs. Pierrepont.

Clemens pushes Nell and Mrs. G out the door. Gerhardt is outside.

GERHARDT   The rights to the mask—that's all I want.

Clemens slams the door.

CLEMENS   Harrison, tell the general—General, listen to this man—

USG   No no.

CLEMENS   What is Cold Harbor?

USG   What is Cold Harbor?

Fred is in a corner of the room, eating his chocolate cake.

FRED Cold Harbor was a disastrous battle in Virginia—Cold Harbor was a turning point in the war.

THE EMPEROR OF JAPAN That you commanded?

CLEMENS That he commanded?

FRED Thousands of his own men dead—thousands. A horrible turning point not just in the war—but in the history of war. A battle of great brutality. My father went mad—he sent wave after wave of his own men to their deaths in a blood lust—thousands of men died for nothing. This cake is so good. Father lost more of his own men than any enemy general could have slain. He was vain and proud. It was a disgrace.

CLEMENS Why isn't that in the book?

FRED Because he's never mentioned it.

CLEMENS Harrison, you were at Cold Harbor?

HARRISON I'd better go. There are guests downstairs—

CLEMENS Were you at Cold Harbor?

HARRISON I was.

CLEMENS Will you tell him about it? Prod his memory.

USG No.

HARRISON I've never spoken of it.

USG No need. No need.

CLEMENS You're disturbed. I believe you might be recollecting. Is this the stimulus? Harrison, go on.

HARRISON I was at Cold Harbor. I can still hear the officers yelling "Charge! Charge!" The men lunged forward. Charge! The men fell dead. Charge! Over and over. The new men cannot get on the battlefield. They climb up the pile of corpses and are shot dead. Charge! The newest soldiers stop. We can't get into the battle. The entries to the field are clogged by bodies. Then climb up the bodies! Charge!

USG No—no.

USG covers his ears.

CLEMENS Sir, listen to him. Is this what's stopping you from writing? The horror of this?

THE EMPRESS OF JAPAN When I am shamed by something, I blot it out. I stop remembering.

THE EMPEROR OF JAPAN I do the same thing.

Nell comes in.

NELL A calling card from—

CLEMENS We are working! It's easier to negotiate the entire Trojan War than write a book in New York City.

USG stops. Mrs. G runs in.

MRS. G Lyss, look! It's Cyrus Keppler from Galena! What friends you were.

USG No no.

CLEMENS We're working.

MRS. G But Cyrus has come all the way.

USG No—no—

87

NELL   Father, to meet people from your past! Father—if you want stimulus—this'll help him remember!

Clemens throws his pencil in the air.

MRS. G   Lyss, don't bring up the fight you had over that election. He didn't vote for you the second time and he told you so and you wanted to punch him in the nose for being a traitor.

Nell shows in THE FALSE CYRUS, *who stands in the doorway carrying a salesman's suitcase. He has an amazing head of hair.*

NELL   Cyrus Keppler. Galena.

CLEMENS   All right—Harrison, don't move—welcome, Mr. Keppler—perhaps we can ask you some questions to joggle the general's—

MRS. G   Who are you?

THE FALSE CYRUS   I sent up my card.

MRS. G   Yes, but it's Cyrus Keppler's.

CLEMENS   Isn't this—

MRS. G   You're not Cyrus Keppler—you're an imposter!

THE FALSE CYRUS   I met old Cyrus on the railroad last winter and he bragged that he knew the general and he gave me his card and he said if you're ever in New York City go look up my friend and tell him Cyrus Keppler sent you and he'll sit you down. So here I am and I'd like to sit down. Did you steal that money from Vanderbilt? Sure is stuffy in here.

MRS. G   Get out.

CLEMENS   You have to leave.

The False Cyrus opens his salesman's case with a flourish. It's filled with rows of bottles and American flags. He takes out one, two, three bottles and begins juggling them.

THE FALSE CYRUS   I'm a seller of hair tonic and if you're unhappy with the amount of your hair, let me tell you what—Hello, sir—oh, he looks sick. This hair tonic has also cured epilepsy in some states. It might work.

CLEMENS   Get out!

MRS. G   You have to leave.

THE FALSE CYRUS (*Closing his case*)   If he's too grand to remember his old friends then I feel sorry for him. He could have a head of hair this thick and bushy—take ten years off his life. (*To USG, loud*) I'm sorry you're dying. It's made everybody forget what a rotten president you were. What a crook you turned into. But now you're a great man all over again. I wanted to buy your book. But I heard you're dying and won't finish it.

CLEMENS   Never pass up a sale. You're mistaken; the book will be finished. For nine dollars, you can have the two-volume set in pure calfskin. For five dollars, you can have your copy bound in leather, and for three-fifty, well, boards and glue.

THE FALSE CYRUS   No no—

CLEMENS   Did you fight in the war?

THE FALSE CYRUS   Thirty-third Regiment out of Illinois!

CLEMENS   This is your valiant leader. Show him your love.

THE FALSE CYRUS   Well, maybe one copy. Three-fifty?

CLEMENS   Better than nothing.

Nell steps up.

NELL   Surely you have a wife.

THE FALSE CYRUS   A beautiful wife with a great head of hair.

NELL   Beautiful wives love to read about epic events in which their hero played a part.

THE FALSE CYRUS   I'll take another one for her.

NELL   Make it calfskin. Show her you care.

CLEMENS   Mrs. Sartoris—

NELL   And on the road so much you must enjoy a lady friend. Carry a few extra copies.

CLEMENS   Mrs. Sartoris, could you do your business downstairs?

The False Cyrus packs up his bag with a flourish.

THE FALSE CYRUS (*To Nell*)   You're good! Would you like to come work for me?

NELL   I might be forced to.

FRED   Sir! Is it hard to sell hair tonic?

MRS. G (*To Clemens*)   And you call yourself a businessman?

Fred, Nell, Mrs. G, and The False Cyrus go. Gerhardt looks in.

GERHARDT   He'll find the strips of plaster very cooling—

Clemens shuts the door. He turns to Harrison.

CLEMENS   Harrison, please.

THE EMPEROR OF JAPAN   Please!

USG   No. No.

HARRISON   Days and days—the heat—the poisoned water.

USG   No.

HARRISON   Charge! The bodies fall. We can't get out on the field to clear the wounded, much less the dead. Thousands of men dying. Charge! Charge! The men fall. A mountain of flesh. The shooting won't stop. Who's running this battle? Ulysses S. Grant. Unconditional Surrender Grant. Men climb up the wall of bodies. Charge! Grant is wasting his men. We are killing our own men—

CLEMENS (*To USG*)   Listen to this—

THE EMPEROR OF JAPAN (*To USG*)   Listen to this—

HARRISON   I pick up a white flag and run up that mountain. Cease fire! In the name of everything good, cease fire! Me at Cold Harbor waving that flag. That's as close to God as I ever came. Or as close as God ever came to me.

USG   Not I. Not I.

HARRISON   I only waved my flag for a few moments. I was shot. In India they put their dead in the rivers. I didn't have to go to India to see that! There was darkness. There must have been a cease-fire because the nurses and soldiers who were alive threw us thousands of corpses into wagons to take us and burn us . . . Well, one of those corpses came to and crawled out from under a stack of corpses—a corpse called *me*. My eyes and ears and nose opened all at once and I thought I was in a butcher's abattoir from the stink of flesh, the taste of blood—not my blood, but other people's blood that had seeped into my mouth. I feel the weight of the flesh, corpses twitch in rigor mortis over me, under me. I hear the groaning of the dead all over me, beside me. I thought dead would be quiet but we were bumping over stones on the way to the fire. Air moving out of corpses. I moved my fingers. I was not dead. The man over me.

Under me. The right of me. The left of me. They were dead. Was I one of them? How had I stayed alive? I must have eaten the flesh around me. Drunk the blood around me for water. I can smell smoke. Flesh. They were burning corpses. They had to. Not enough earth on this earth to bury all this dead. Scoop up all the sand in the Sahara, collect all the dirt of the steppes of Russia—not enough earth to cover all these Cold Harbor dead. But I am not one of them! Don't put me in fire! I pushed my way up through the weight of stinking flesh. Was dying like being born? My hand reached out of the dead wagon and grabbed a soldier by the arm. He saw my eyes open and he screamed loud— "Stop the wagon!" The moving wagon stopped. "Don't put me in fire. Not fire! I am not dead. I swear." Soldiers prodded me with a bayonet. "Do you think the black one's telling the truth?" My lips moved. "I'm telling the truth." They pulled me out of the flesh the way you'd rescue a drowning swimmer out of the sea. How many more men were alive in those wagons headed to the flames? We have to live for them. Are we still in that death wagon struggling to get out from under that ton of corpses?

USG   Did we all die at Cold Harbor? Is this life? Are you alive? Did I dream you?

THE EMPEROR OF JAPAN   All those men dead?

USG   I sent them all out to die. For days. Thousands.

THE EMPEROR OF JAPAN   Were you drunk?

USG   Of course I was drunk. You have to be drunk to let thousands of men die. But it was the only choice I had. To end the war. All those crowds outside the window—they're the spirits of all those men. I can't make money writing about those men's deaths. All the men die. I can't rescue

92

myself financially by writing about all those men I led to their deaths.

THE EMPEROR OF JAPAN   You remembered.

CLEMENS   You remembered.

USG   Is that what memory is? This rotten taste in my mouth? I thought it was the cancer. Is this what memory tastes like? Do you have a drink?

Clemens pours him a glass of brandy. USG drinks.

THE EMPEROR OF JAPAN   Why did the South last so long? Why did the South fight? Were they all fighting for slavery? They weren't all slaveholders. It's not why the South lost. How did they hold on so long? Why did it take you so long? Why? Was Cold Harbor your last straw?

USG   Burn . . . Fire . . . worth it . . .

THE EMPEROR OF JAPAN   You couldn't take it that they might win? That's why you had to sacrifice your own men—to cover up your own failure, that they had won for too long. They had outwitted you—fewer men—less money—yet they kept winning and they would have won Cold Harbor but you sacrificed your own men, hundreds of your own men, thousands of your own men, a mountain of your own men. That's what Cold Harbor was—it showed you what you were.

THE EMPRESS OF JAPAN   It was worth it. The Union survived. Slavery's ended.

THE EMPEROR OF JAPAN   You had two ideas. Save the Union. End slavery. You never swayed from those two imperatives. That's why I love you. That's why I stepped forward and shook your hand. That's why I'm here today. I don't care

93

what happened with Vanderbilt. That's money. Money can always be replaced. But nations can't be replaced. Things like slavery don't wither away. They have to be assaulted. No matter the cost. These are very dangerous thoughts in my country.

USG   Clemens, I owe you a book.

CLEMENS   Harrison, remind me to give you a million dollars—

HARRISON   Will he write about Cold Harbor? If he doesn't, the book is worthless. It'll make my life worthless.

CLEMENS   How is that?

HARRISON   I wanted to kill this man, which is why I took the position as his valet. When they first told me of my new post, I said no—then I said yes—to answer the voices in my head—all the voices who died at Cold Harbor saying I want revenge. I would kill him in his bath—in his bed. But this family never leaves him alone! I stayed with him waiting for my chance at revenge. And then one day I realized it wasn't up to me to seek vengeance. He was fighting to end slavery. He had to bring the nation together. He had two ideas, that's all. He needed the men at Cold Harbor to wear down the other side. I was spared. No more vengeance. I've been happy to be with him the last few years—to be this close to history—to greatness—to see his sadness—his bravery. He punishes himself. I still wish I had killed him.

USG   It was *you* that wanted to kill me. I knew someone did.

HARRISON   What will you say about Cold Harbor?

USG   Can't write that. Can't make money off that kind of memory . . .

CLEMENS Is that why you can't remember? General, it's your duty to tell the truth—

USG No.

CLEMENS The truth.

HARRISON The reason we have such regard for the truth is we have so little opportunity to get familiar with it.

CLEMENS I like that.

He makes a note of it. Sounds of commotion. Buck appears.

BUCK You will never believe who is here.

USG rails.

CLEMENS You've done enough damage to your father!

Fred runs in.

FRED You have no right to be here.

BUCK Father! Don't move—adjust—pushing through the crowds I saw a familiar face—I couldn't believe it—look who's come to see you! To stand outside in the crowds and wish you well—Look! Father! Who is the greatest opera singer in the world? Adelina Patti is here!

The great woman, ADELINA PATTI, appears.

PATTI I come to give you the gift of life! I will dedicate my *next* farewell concert to the general. You all must come and then come backstage! I retire. The world salutes me. I salute him. I don't care if he's a crook! I am here. I wear black because I am your widow—

Mrs. G strides in, angry.

MRS. G Move on, lady.

CLEMENS Good God!

PATTI But that is Mark Twain? All the immortal people know each other. This is Mount Olympus. I bow to you and you and me! Do you like opera?

CLEMENS I must. I've seen the first act of just about every one ever written.

BUCK She's retired. This glorious voice will never be heard again.

CLEMENS Didn't you say farewell three weeks ago?

PATTI Memory—that most fragile of organs—is the only way I'll stay alive. I need you there to remember me. Greatness needs greatness.

MRS. G He cannot accept your kind invitation.

PATTI But I need great people in my audience to remember my great voice.

BUCK Father, she'll dedicate the concert to you.

PATTI See me as I am about to fade away into the misty glen of memory. See your people? Your people are my people.

Patti opens the curtains onto the dark street. The crowd roars.

USG All my soldiers, going off to die. Close that curtain!

The power in USG's voice makes Patti close the curtains.

BUCK We'll remember you forever—come sing! Let him hear you sing. That's the only medicine Father needs. Take more flowers. These are yours.

Buck fills Patti's arms with flowers, as Patti sings "The Last Rose of Summer":

PATTI   'Tis the last rose of summer
Left blooming alone
All her lovely companions
Have faded and gone
No flower of her kindred
No rosebud is nigh
To reflect back her blushes
Or give her sigh for sigh

CLEMENS   (*Overlapping the song, to us*)   I have to get this man
out of here! I'll take him to Elmira. I have a farm in
Elmira—he can stay there—until he finishes. I'll get him
out of this house. It is impossible to work in New York.
You can live in New York and be a witness in New York,
but you can't live in New York and write!

HARRISON   What will he say about Cold Harbor?

USG   Can't . . . no. Can't make money off that kind of
memory . . .

CLEMENS   Sir, it's the truth—

Badeau enters, limping as always.

BADEAU   Up! Up! Out! Salvation! We are saved—everybody
out!

PATTI   Good-bye good-bye.

Patti leaves, dispensing kisses to all, to the air.

BUCK   Don't go!

Buck follows Patti out.

CLEMENS   You've done enough harm.

Nell runs in with a suitcase.

97

NELL Badeau will save us!

BADEAU How's the book coming? Looks the same measly height it was when I was here. Pack each stack of pages in a separate box. Pack up! We are on the run! Dose him for a trip.

MRS. G You can't order us out of our own house in the middle of the night—

NELL Listen to Badeau! We're saved!

BADEAU I am saving the day—no, the day *and* the night and forever!

CLEMENS I'll call the police.

Harrison runs in, followed by a desolate Buck.

HARRISON Who are those men downstairs packing the trunks?

BADEAU The sailors on the ship that takes us to Utopia. Pack these pages carefully. Wrap them in canvas.

BUCK Signora Patti is gone!

FRED Utopia means nowhere.

BUCK Doesn't anyone care?

BADEAU The money we find there will make Utopia real. You will live in financial Eden! Death is the only thing trying to kill you. We shall outwit the grim reaper!

BUCK What's wrong with you people!

NELL Mother, listen to Badeau!

BADEAU Hurry hurry! I have left you to stew in your juices long enough. Face the fact. He's never going to finish his book. There is never going to be money. You need money.

His memory is gone. I have recognized his one remaining asset. His death. I have sold the rights to his *death!*

MRS. G   He's not going to die!

CLEMENS   You're selling his death?

BADEAU   Absolutely. Look at all those people standing outside his house. All across America the word of his impending death that *I* released absolves him into innocence. Where this man dies will become a tourist mecca! Americans love to travel to a happy place but they need a serious purpose.

CLEMENS   Where are you taking him?

FRED   You can't uproot us.

MRS. G   You can't make us refugees.

NELL   You do have to tell us where we're going. I have to leave word for my husband where I'll be. Suppose he arrives. He can't come to an empty house.

CLEMENS   Tell us!

BADEAU   Tell this crew of flannelmouths, who'll broadcast it to the treetops? If the horde of creditors knew the general was leaving town they'd build a Wall of China around this house.

USG   Are we going to Japan?

BADEAU   No one is to know. Not till he's safe at sea. Pack everything you need.

NELL   Mother, don't be difficult.

MRS. G   I'm not leaving.

BADEAU Then stay here in the poverty of your lives. Where will you live? The house will be gone. What will you live on when this man dies? All right all right. I tried my best to make your fortune and to protect your father. (*Calls*) Crew! Stop packing their belongings. I resign.

CLEMENS We are staying here.

BADEAU You're in charge? Fine. Shall I give them the order? Stay in New York trying to whittle out an impossible book? Or sail off to financial paradise? What should I instruct these sailors?

MRS. G What kind of money?

BADEAU A Niagara Falls of money. The place to which I take you is giving us its three most magnificent houses, each next to the other. There is no telegraph where I'm taking you. No one will know he is there. You will have many servants to do your bidding. He will finish his days in peace. Isn't that what you want? And then after the mournful event which awaits all of us—the tourists, the pilgrims will begin arriving.

BUCK Mother, don't let him bully you. New York would never let us down.

CLEMENS (*To us*) America is the ultimate democracy. Anyone can end up in the gutter. (*To Badeau*) Is this true?

BADEAU Oh, it's true. Listen to me. When the general dies, you will run the house where he died as a museum.

MRS. G I could never sell that privacy—

BADEAU You'll get used to it. Buy a ticket to see the very bed where the general died! You will sell drinking cups with his face on them, three-dimensional opticons of scenes from his life, authentic Civil War army hats. Picture postal cards. Mezzotints of Civil War scenes, lithographs, key chains and get fifty percent of the net. Plus I will edit these fragments of his memoirs and bind them into a special edition.

CLEMENS I'm the publisher!

BADEAU Not the only publisher. These people on the street are your future. Multiply their love by tens of thousands. Their devotion to their leader will prove a bottomless seven seas of money, flinging up gorgeous waves of gold. The town fathers of my destination are being very generous. Before that influx of pilgrims arrives, with your new house as collateral, you will buy up property at rock-bottom prices. You will own the island and put up no money.

MRS. G The island? What island?

NELL Is it Newport? I hope it's Newport. My husband has friends at Newport.

BADEAU Newport is in the business of keeping people out, not bringing tourists in!

BUCK Go down south! Charleston, South Carolina! I have friends in Charleston.

MRS. G No. I will not let him go to enemy territory. They're still fighting the war down there.

FRED Bar Harbor—Maine—I bet Maine.

MRS. G Where did they take Napoleon?

BADEAU St. Helena.

MRS. G Not St. Helena—not where he died—the first exile—

CLEMENS Elba—

MRS. G We're going to the American Elba? Exile—oh God—where?

BADEAU You will then use that property as collateral to build the hotels to house the pilgrims. You will then lease the ships that bring pilgrims to the shrine. You can even build the ships if you want to. You'll get a share of the ticket sales. The ships. The restaurants. The hotels. The sunshine. The very air.

CLEMENS Are you in on the take?

BADEAU Of course I'm in on the take. I smell money, my tail goes up. Oh, good God, everybody will make money. Except you, Mr. Clemens.

FRED Seeing the shrine where my father died is not my idea of a sufficient attraction.

BADEAU Which is why I have contacted Mr. Phineas T. Barnum, who will open a whaling museum where you can see the sights around the world that the whalers saw. The South Seas. Dark-skinned, nude, naked native girls dancing authentic pagan rituals. Wild men of Borneo, untouched by time, spitting in Darwin's face. Adelina Patti? This time next year you'll be sitting in your house on Main Street dining with Signora Patti and P. T. Barnum before her debut in the new opera house. Do you know Madame Tussaud?

MRS. G Is that a brothel?

BADEAU Artistry in wax. The general will live for eternity in wax. Bow low to your salvation. Inject him. Prepare him for the journey. You'll own it all. Thanks to your son, you've lost all your money. Thanks to me, the general will leave you a fortune. Selling tickets to the dreamers of small dreams who want to see the man who had large dreams.

MRS. G (*To us*)   I never dreamed small dreams. I married my Victor. That's what I call him, after King Victor Immanuel of Italy. Now there was a dream.

NELL (*To us*)   I didn't dream small. I married a man this close to the nobility. He dreamed big dreams. He thought I had money.

BUCK (*To us*)   I didn't dream small. I dreamed I could start an investment bank. I just got involved with a man who dreamed illegal dreams. I do dream of opera. That makes me enormous.

FRED (*To us*)   I never dreamed at all. I have lived under his shadow. I never minded. It's very cool and comforting living under his shadow.

HARRISON (*To us*)   I have dreams, but they're nobody's business but my own.

Gerhardt opens the door.

GERHARDT (*To us*)   I never dreamed small. My statue of the general will be the most famous statue in the world. The Colossus of Rhodes.

Gerhardt shuts the door.

CLEMENS (*To us*)   I never dreamed small. But by God I don't want to die small . . .

BADEAU   We leave at midnight.

CLEMENS   It's a shame you didn't handle the death of our Lord. Jesus settled for so little.

BADEAU Perhaps I got the deal for Matthew, Mark, Luke, and John to write the Gospels. Yes! In another life I published the Bible. And wrote parts of it. In another life I did get the idea for Christ to come back to life. In this life I got the idea that if it can be done with one savior, why not the savior of another? Yes, I remember now. It all comes back to me. Yes! I did handle the death of Christ. Christ listened to me. Christ wasn't like you. After the island is restored to its primacy, you can sell the property at enormous profits and go wherever your fortune takes you. Open the curtains. Look out in the street! When the general is dead, that's who'll come to Nantucket.

MRS. G Nantucket?

BADEAU Nantucket. I've told you. I trust you.

NELL Isn't that fishermen?

FRED (*To Mrs. G*) Nantucket? You went there twelve years ago.

MRS. G We did? Giant figures carved in stone?

FRED That was Abu Simbel.

MRS. G Nantucket?

FRED Flat. Bleak.

MRS. G We've been around the world. Nantucket? We're supposed to swoon?

USG Nantan.

MRS. G Nantucket.

USG Where?

THE EMPRESS OF JAPAN (*Reading from a guidebook*) "Nantucket Island, thirty miles at sea, of great geological interest, is the only part of America not connected underwater to the continental landmass. The Ice Age cut a path between Nantucket and the mainland. Nantucket is completely isolated."

MRS. G   There must be another place besides Nantucket.

BADEAU   Nantucket is making us secure. Prepare him for the journey.

CLEMENS   Secure? Listen to me. Stay here. I can get the book out of him. He's finished enough for one volume. I have already sold so many copies—don't give up on him.

FRED   Give my father peace.

NELL   Mother, I don't know what to say.

BADEAU   The choice is very clear.

MRS. G   You're sure it's a fortune?

BADEAU   Shakespeare says it in *The Tempest*. People who wouldn't give a penny to a poor man will pay ten to see a dead Indian.

CLEMENS   Goddamn Shakespeare. Right again.

MRS. G   Ulysses is hardly a dead Indian.

BADEAU   But happily of even more curiosity. What should I instruct the crew?

CLEMENS   Please give me one last try at the book. I have faith in—

MRS. G   I love you, Mr. Clemens, but this time we have to listen to Mr.—I hate even to say his name—Badeau. Bad water. Bathwater. A diet of bad bathwater.

FRED   No choice. Sail to Nantucket.

BADEAU Onward?

MRS. G Yes, onward, with Mr. Bad Bathwater.

NELL & BUCK Onward!

BADEAU We catch the midnight tide! Down to the docks!

Nell, Fred, and Buck go off.

MRS. G Leave our home. Gallop through the night. The only lights will be the ones streaming out of opium dens. Gin mills. Brothels. The streets will reel with drunkards. Painted women will reach up to the carriage to grab us—I'm not leaving!

BADEAU (*To USG*) —and do you know how we travel? The ship to Nantucket is your old ship, the *River Queen*—you'll recognize this ship.

USG River Queen.

BADEAU You used it in the war as your dispatch ship. You sailed up and down the James River—to City Point—the memories will flow—

USG To Cold Harbor?

BADEAU Yes, it delivered you to Cold Harbor.

USG No Cold Harbor.

MRS. G That foul ship—the ash. The horrible grim smell of coal. Volcanic ash will come down and coat us. What was that volcano that destroyed—you know—

USG Fujiyama. Asama-yama.

MRS. G No. Pompeii. Yes—remember that time we went to Pompeii? To see fossils of those people frozen in their tracks. Suffocated with ash. They thought the day would be another day—a bright day—a sweet day. This man can hardly breathe and you'd bring him onto that dark ship?

BADEAU The *River Queen* now lives as the ferry on and off Nantucket.

CLEMENS Memory come to take you to memory.

BADEAU A very winning phrase. We can use that in the souvenir brochure.

MRS. G Oh Lyss, I thought in New York we'd be safe from kidnappers, yet here we are, snatched out of our home and shipped off to some strange faraway plantation like slaves snatched off the beaches of Africa. Is our destination Africa? That would be the final irony. The man who fought to end slavery becomes a slave.

Nell, Buck, and Fred appear with suitcases, dressed for travel.

NELL Good-bye heartless New York.

FRED Good-bye brutal New York.

BUCK Why why why do we leave this magic place?

BADEAU No money no money no money. We have to go out the back way. No creditor must witness our flight. I've ordered carriages to come around back and take us to the docks.

MRS. G Let us go in the street. I just want to catch one last look at freedom before we—

BADEAU No one must see you with your suitcase. No one must know we're gone. Give him a dose. Prepare this man for travel.

Mrs. G checks her timepiece.

MRS. G   Fifty-eight. Fifty-nine. Sixty. And now it's time for his medicine.

FRED   One last look at freedom before we sail out onto the River Styx.

NELL   This river is the river right in to hell.

FRED   New York will go by.

BUCK   The cruel sun will rise to show us what we're leaving.

MRS. G   The morphine goes into his veins.

THE EMPEROR OF JAPAN   See the candlelight catch the silver tip of a needle.

THE EMPRESS OF JAPAN   The needle goes into the old man's arm.

THE EMPEROR OF JAPAN   The morphine flows into your vein.

BUCK   Adelina Patti—to hear you once more.

Mrs. G injects. Patti appears and sings.

PATTI   O Happy Isle on the ocean's breast
        The ships are idle; thy commerce dead
        But the angel of health "sits up aloft"
        And sheds a halo o'er thy head

THE EMPEROR OF JAPAN   I am the throne of chrysanthemum.

USG   And I am come to Japan to see you.

THE EMPEROR OF JAPAN   We are the two most powerful men in the world.

USG   If I could stay here forever.

THE EMPEROR OF JAPAN   I'm flattered. He wants to stay here with us—

USG Was being with you the last time I was ever happy? Yes. You wanted nothing from me. We were the two most powerful men in the world. Who are we now? Save me.

THE EMPEROR OF JAPAN How?

USG Save me.

THE EMPEROR OF JAPAN I can't do anything. My priests do for me.

THE EMPRESS OF JAPAN Do something!

THE EMPEROR OF JAPAN I am the throne of chrysanthemum. I am—

THE EMPRESS OF JAPAN Help him. We will lose him. When you stepped forward to shake his hand it was the most courageous thing anyone has ever done. I loved you. Be that man. Do one courageous thing.

The Emperor and Empress of Japan vanish.

USG Don't leave me!

Harrison runs in.

HARRISON Sir, look out the window. Wait till you see that carriage coming through the crowds. You'll recognize that livery! Do you know who it is? It is Mr. William Henry Vanderbilt!

Nell, Fred, and Buck go to the window.

NELL His carriage couldn't be coming here—pushing his way through the crowds—

MRS. G The coachman must have made a wrong turn.

NELL The carriage slows down.

MRS. G Lyss! The carriage is stopping! Oh God—

FRED The footman hops down from the back of Vanderbilt's carriage.

MRS. G The footman opens the coach door—

NELL A man's leg sticks out—now the other—

BUCK The body follows—

NELL The head lifts—

MRS. G It can't be—it is. Lyss, it's Mr. William Henry Vanderbilt!

FRED Where is he going?

NELL He couldn't be coming here—

BUCK He is! He walks to our stairs.

MRS. G I know—he's come to demand his money. He wants to insult us. He wants to slap your face. He's going to say I trusted you—I voted for you twice—you were my hero—and then you stole one hundred and fifty thousand dollars from me. I know he's going to say that. Oh Lyss, prepare yourself. It's the worst humiliation.

A loud door knock.

MRS. G Open the door—let him in—someone.

HARRISON Mr. William Henry Vanderbilt.

The Emperor of Japan enters, carrying a large cane, dressed as a businessman, but all in white with a bright gold vest.

USG You came!

EMPEROR/VANDERBILT First, I have talked to my friends in Congress. A great oversight is being remedied. The general's pension is being instated.

MRS. G Lyss!

EMPEROR/VANDERBILT It has also come to my attention you need to write your memoirs in a quiet place—

BADEAU He's not writing his memoirs. He's going to die.

EMPEROR/VANDERBILT Mr. Clemens, can you produce the memoirs?

CLEMENS Yes!

EMPEROR/VANDERBILT Mr. Badeau. Go!

BADEAU Sir, let me stay. He needs me. These people, they are nothing without me—

Emperor/Vanderbilt pounds his stick with great echoing force.

CLEMENS But we need quiet. We need freedom from financial woes.

EMPEROR/VANDERBILT I'll take care of the financial woes. My friend, Mr. Drexel, has a place of tranquility in the Adirondacks. Mount MacGregor. I will send you in my railroad car—

BADEAU I have made a deal! You can't take him away! He is mine!

Emperor/Vanderbilt pounds his stick with great echoing force and glares at Badeau with his imperial power. Badeau crumbles.

BADEAU Yessir. Whatever you say. Whatever you say. Whatever you say.

Badeau goes.

EMPEROR/VANDERBILT I will settle your immediate debts.

USG I owe you one hundred and fifty thousand dollars.

EMPEROR/VANDERBILT All the more reason for you to finish your book and pay me. I shan't forgive that debt. You must write your book and pay me back. To do that you will need a proper nurse. I present you with the greatest nurse and stenographer in the business. She will be your muse.

The Empress of Japan enters dressed as a nurse.

EMPRESS/NURSE Get your muses straight. I am not your muse. If I am anyone, I am Memory and memory was never a muse. Memory is the mother of all the muses. Memory is a goddess. You must be careful never to lose me. Treat me with respect. Lose me and the world loses its memory. I am Order. I am Memory. Call me by my Mount Olympus name. Call me Mnemosyne. Let us recollect.

USG smiles and reaches out to her.

USG "My family is American, and has been for generations, in all branches, direct and collateral."

FRED He remembers!

USG Of course I remember you. Forgive me. I didn't know.

EMPEROR/VANDERBILT I forgive you. You look warm—try this fan—

Emperor/Vanderbilt produces a golden fan, which he gives to USG.

USG I have it back!

EMPEROR/VANDERBILT Keep it this time.

EMPRESS/NURSE I will now give him the proper medication.

MRS. G I see her plan. These nurses all think they can come in and supplant me.

FRED Mother, this is now the nurse's domain. She is his memory. Let us retrospect.

MRS. G Made an exile in my own home by a muse with a hypodermic syringe. I take care of him. Don't think you can supplant me. You're not the first nurse to come in here with her dreams—

EMPRESS/NURSE Has this man been baptized?

MRS. G No!

USG No!

EMPRESS/NURSE Be quiet. Let her have what she wants.

USG My baptism—do you truly want that?

MRS. G Yes. I don't want to lose you through eternity because you're a pagan.

EMPRESS/NURSE He's a minister.

EMPEROR/VANDERBILT In my very own church.

MRS. G Are you a little bit close to the Methodists?

EMPRESS/NURSE Say you are.

EMPEROR/VANDERBILT Absolutely.

Emperor/Vanderbilt shakes water over USG, baptizing him. Golden light. Mrs. G weeps with joy. Patti sings Beethoven's "Ode to Joy" from the Ninth Symphony.

EMPRESS/NURSE Let us recollect.

USG "Although frequently urged by friends to write my memoirs, I had determined never to do so, nor to write anything for publication. At the age of nearly sixty-two, I received an injury from a fall, which confined me closely to the house."

MRS. G Don't mention the cancer! This is a happy book. Cancer—I said the word.

USG "Confined me closely to the house, while it did not apparently affect my general health."

MRS. G That's better. It's nobody's business to know. Mr. Vanderbilt, we'll send you the first copy of the book.

EMPEROR/VANDERBILT No need to. You see, I don't read.

MRS. G Really?

CLEMENS The Adirondacks, is it?

Gerhardt runs in.

GERHARDT The death mask!

EMPEROR/VANDERBILT Travel with us.

GERHARDT You'll give me the rights?

USG But wait till I'm dead.

GERHARDT Thank you.

EMPRESS/NURSE Let us recollect.

Patti stops singing. USG takes a piece of paper and writes.

EMPEROR/VANDERBILT We travel in my railroad car up along the Hudson River into the Adirondacks.

USG You forgive me? For giving your fan away—

EMPEROR/VANDERBILT I have to forgive you. We are the two most powerful men in the world.

CLEMENS (*To us*) A miracle occurs. In spite of unendurable pain, he perseveres. He writes his book. The pages flow out of him. He writes two hundred pages more than expected.

USG speaks in a very clear voice.

USG (*To us*) "The war has made us a nation of great power and intelligence. We have but little to do to preserve peace, happiness, and prosperity at home, and the respect of other nations. Our experience ought to teach us the necessity of the first; our power secures the latter. I feel that we are on the eve of a new era, when there is to be great harmony between the Federal and Confederate. I cannot stay to be a living witness to the correctness of this prophecy; but I feel it within me that it is to be so. The universally kind feeling expressed for me, at a time when it was supposed that each day would prove my last, seemed to me the beginning of the answer to 'Let us have peace.'"

THE EMPEROR OF JAPAN You died July twenty-third, 1885.

THE EMPRESS OF JAPAN Your last words were purported to be—

USG Water . . .

His head drops. His pen and pages fall to the ground. Gerhardt lays strips of wet white gauze over his face.

CLEMENS Five months later, by the tenth of December, I had shipped out three hundred and twenty-five thousand copies of the book. Mrs. Grant received a first check of two hundred thousand dollars, which was twice the previous record for the largest royalty check ever paid.

MRS. G The second check was for a hundred and fifty thousand dollars. I handed the check to Mr. Vanderbilt. He handed it right back to me.

CLEMENS At one time, one out of every three families in America owned a copy of his memoirs. If I paid him his royalties in silver dollars, the weight would be seventeen tons.

GERHARDT   The family allowed me into his bedroom. I took the death mask. (*Gerhardt removes the gauze and produces the death mask. They all take it and hold it and pass it along.*) My hands did not tremble. I cast it in bronze. I'd make my fortune by producing copies when—

MRS. G   We stopped it! There is no contract! We are not peddling the general's death mask.

GERHARDT   I ended life in New Orleans as a tailor and a bartender.

MRS. G (*To us*)   Everybody did very well out of the book.

CLEMENS (*To us*)   The lack of money is the root of all evil.

THE EMPEROR OF JAPAN (*To us*)   Except Samuel Clemens. He invested his profits back into his publishing company.

THE EMPRESS OF JAPAN (*To us*)   It went bankrupt in 1894. Poor Mark Twain.

USG stands.

USG   Will I be remembered?

THE EMPEROR OF JAPAN   Mainly as a joke. Who's buried in Grant's tomb?

USG   What's the answer?

THE EMPEROR OF JAPAN   You are. And later—your wife.

USG   Julia will be with me? I'm glad she'll be with me. But will I be remembered?

THE EMPEROR OF JAPAN   As money. Your face on a bill.

USG   Low currency? Fives? Ones?

THE EMPEROR OF JAPAN Higher than Lincoln or Washington. You're on the fifty.

USG So I'm not that popular.

THE EMPEROR OF JAPAN Things will get more expensive. You'll be remembered.

USG My memoirs? What did people say about them?

THE EMPEROR OF JAPAN William Dean Howells said, "The general is one of the best writers I have ever read." A writer named Gertrude Stein will say:

THE EMPRESS OF JAPAN "I have just found the two volumes of Grant's *Memoirs* and have just bought them to read again . . . I always wanted to collaborate with someone about General Grant . . . as if he might have been Hiram Grant instead of Ulysses Grant and what a difference that would have made."

USG Did Matthew Arnold ever change his mind?

Badeau enters, reading.

BADEAU Even my great friend Matthew Arnold finally said he found "a language straightforward, nervous, firm, possessing . . . the high merit of saying clearly in the fewest possible words what had to be said and saying it . . . with shrewd and unexpected turns of expression."

The False Cyrus enters, reading.

THE FALSE CYRUS Edmund Wilson will say, "The writing in the memoirs is perfect in concision and clearness, in its propriety and purity of language."

USG So it was worth it?

THE EMPEROR OF JAPAN Worth it? If Shakespeare hadn't written one word or Beethoven one note, there still would've been the war between the States. There still would've been Cold Harbor.

MRS. G Nothing about Cold Harbor—

HARRISON Sir. One statement about Cold Harbor. Put those men's souls to rest.

USG "I have always regretted that the last assault at Cold Harbor was ever made. At Cold Harbor no advantage whatever was gained to compensate for the heavy loss we sustained."

HARRISON Sir, can you say more?

USG That's all there'll be about Cold Harbor.

MRS. G That's all there'll be about Cold Harbor.

HARRISON Then that will have to do. That will be in the book?

USG Yes.

HARRISON Thank you.

USG Are you remembered?

THE EMPEROR OF JAPAN Mainly as an operetta.

A gramophone appears, playing a recording of The Mikado: *"If you want to know who we are, we are gentlemen of Japan." The Empress of Japan angrily drags the needle across the record to shut it off.*

USG —and Clemens?

THE EMPEROR OF JAPAN   A writer named Ernest Hemingway will say every American novel is descended from *Huckleberry Finn.*

CLEMENS (*To us*)   I'll be truthful: I could live on compliments.

USG   My family?

THE EMPEROR OF JAPAN   Mrs. Grant stays in New York and becomes best friends with Mrs. Jefferson Davis, the widow of the president of the Confederacy.

NELL   Nell will leave her husband and move to America to be with her.

USG   Not surprised. The boys?

FRED   Fred will become police commissioner of New York City.

BUCK   Buck will move to California where he'll run for senator. He will lose.

USG   And Badeau?

BADEAU   I will go on to write the definitive text on the aristocracy in England. I will then die very happily.

Badeau leaves.

USG   And you and I?

THE EMPEROR OF JAPAN   We will have our troubles. We will attack you.

USG   No! Why?

THE EMPEROR OF JAPAN   For all kinds of reasons—and then you will bomb us. Remember Nagasaki?

USG   Gentle Nagasaki.

THE EMPEROR OF JAPAN   You'll destroy that in retaliation, as well as Hiroshima.

USG   Are we enemies?

THE EMPEROR OF JAPAN   We become friends again . . . sort of . . .

He guides USG to his chair.

USG   Where are you taking me?

THE EMPEROR OF JAPAN   To a holy mountain called the Adirondacks, where your spirit will remember and soar with greater ease to this place where I am.

CLEMENS (*To us*)   The Adirondacks gave us a good deal. Shares in the railroad. Lots of money all around—

EMPRESS/NURSE   Let us retrospect.

USG   "The fact is I think I am a verb instead of a personal pronoun. A verb is anything that signifies *to be, to do,* or *to suffer.* I signify all three."

THE EMPEROR OF JAPAN   Write your memories. Set them down. Don't let America forget the war . . . That's all writing a book is: a letter to an unknown friend.

CLEMENS   History is merely the biography of a few stout individuals. You're one of those few individuals. Let us retrospect. The story about the apple tree . . .

THE EMPEROR OF JAPAN   Tell the truth.

THE EMPRESS OF JAPAN   Go on.

THE EMPEROR OF JAPAN   Go on.

MRS. G   Go on.

USG   (*With great difficulty*)   "Wars produce many stories of fiction . . ."

CLEMENS   Good. He'll be fine.

MRS. G   He'll be fine.

THE EMPEROR OF JAPAN   Good. I'm here. You're safe.

USG takes the Emperor's hand. He writes confidently.

CURTAIN